# ONE TOUGH
## Mother

### It's Time to Step Up
### and Be the Mom

## Julie Barnhill

## Revell
Grand Rapids, Michigan

For Becky, Brenda, Reilly, and Suzie.
Your schlecke counsel was just what
One Tough Mother needed.
I love you all more than I can say, almost.

---

© 2007 by Julie Barnhill

Published by Fleming H. Revell
a division of Baker Publishing Group
P.O. Box 6287, Grand Rapids, MI 49516-6287
www.revellbooks.com

Printed in the United States of America

Library of Congress Cataloging-in-Publication Data
Barnhill, Julie Ann, 1965–
        One tough mother : it's time to step up and be the mom / Julie Barnhill.
            p.    cm.
        Includes bibliographical references.
        ISBN 10: 0-8007-3230-8 (pbk.)
        ISBN 978-0-8007-3230-1 (pbk.)
        1. Motherhood—Religious aspects—Christianity. I. Title.
    BV4529.18.B384   2007
    248.8′431—dc22                                                        2007021589

Scripture is taken from the *Holy Bible*, New Living Translation, copyright © 1996. Used by permission of Tyndale House Publishers, Inc., Wheaton, Illinois 60189. All rights reserved.

Scripture marked NASB is taken from the New American Standard Bible®, Copyright © 1960, 1962, 1963, 1968, 1971, 1972, 1973, 1975, 1977, 1995 by The Lockman Foundation. Used by permission.

Published in association with the literary agencies of Alive Communications, Inc., 7680 Goddard Street, Suite 200, Colorado Springs, Colorado 80920, and Fedd & Company, Inc., 9759 Concord Pass, Brentwood, Tennessee 37027.

# Contents

1  Behold! The Power of Murle    5
   *Introducing One Tough Mother*

2  First Things First    13
   *One Tough Mother Basics*

3  Sit Down and Shut Up    27
   *Nonnegotiable #1: Be the Boss (without Apology!)*

4  Diagnosis: Average    55
   *Nonnegotiable #2: Delight in Your Perfectly Ordinary Child*

5  Analyze This    69
   *Nonnegotiable #3: Stop Tinkering with the Inane*

6  Non, Nyet, Nada, Nein, Nulle    79
   *Nonnegotiable #4: Say No Like You Mean It*

7  Scrapbooking: A Woman's Descent into Madness    99
   *Nonnegotiable #5: Get a Hobby Other Than Your Kid*

8  Truly, Madly, Deeply    109
   *Nonnegotiable #6: Love Them Like Crazy*

9 These Things I Know to Be True   125
   *Nonnegotiable #7: Remember It's All Worth It*

10 Just Say It   145
   *Nonnegotiable #8: Leave Nothing Unspoken*

11 My Kingdom for a Slingshot   157
   *Nonnegotiable #9: Face Your Giants*

12 You're Only a Failure If You Quit, Like,
   Forever   179
   *Nonnegotiable #10: Never Give Up*


   Appendix: Maintaining and Accessorizing
      "The Package"   191
   Notes   203
   Acknowledgments   205

# 1

# Behold! The Power of Murle

## Introducing One Tough Mother

Slightly graying hair coupled with a steely gaze and stern voice of certainty—Mrs. Murle Woolston had formidable down to an exact science. As a kid at my friend Angie's house, I knew it was a given that Murle the Mom's Rules would be strictly enforced. And if you were even *mildly* intelligent, you adhered to said Rules willingly and obediently. No questions asked.

Rule #1: During indoor games of hide-and-seek, Murle's bedroom was unequivocally a No-Play Zone.

Rule #2: Hardcover *Encyclopedia Britannica* and accompanying *World Almanacs* (which I found utterly fascinating and loved to read) were to be returned to their appropriate shelf space after use—*pronto*.

Rule #3: The back laundry room door was not to be used for entering or exiting the house; the garage entrance was preferred.

Rule #4: When running through the house . . . uh, wait a minute, running wasn't allowed in Murle's house.

Rule #5: One was never—no, never—allowed to curiously poke objects through the metal grates of the electrical wall heating units inset along the narrow hallway leading to Angie's back bedroom. (And oh, how those mesmerizing coils begged to be prodded with a pencil, toothpick, or plastic-coated hairpin!)

Around age six, I could no longer stave off the temptation to test Rule #5, and I defiantly stuck my right pointer finger through the grate, gleefully making contact with the beckoning glowing metal.

Bad idea.

Not only did I burn myself and wind up crying like a, well, six-year-old, but I had to seek comfort and medical attention from the only adult in the house. (Yes, that would be Murle.)

Holding my hand in hers, Murle carefully dabbed a spot of ointment on the tip of my throbbing finger, then queried with aforementioned stern voice, "Julie, how did you burn your finger?" Trust me on this—never in all my years of playing paper dolls (many of you don't have the slightest clue what I'm referring to, do you?), listening to vinyl 45 records, or playing Twister did it *ever* occur to me to try to pull one over on Angie's mom.

Nope. I told the truth, the whole truth, and nothing but the finger-poking truth.

Amazingly enough, she didn't yell or spank me*—but believe me, I would have preferred ei-

*Not that she ever had, but I did grow up in the prehistoric days when noncustodial adults could and would smack one's backside if warranted. If you are thirty-five years old or younger, place a brown paper bag over your mouth and nose, breathe, and wait until the feeling you will pass out goes away.

ther if it had meant I could get out of the room faster. Gently wrapping a protective Band-Aid around my injury, Murle leaned forward ever so slightly in the chair she was sitting on, locked eyes with me, and declared in that utterly distinctive, gravelly voice of hers, "This won't happen again." And it never did, for even a first grader could deduce the foolishness of messing with Murle.

Thirty-plus years later and I easily recall the Rules, but you know what I can't remember? Murle actually verbalizing any one of them, or for that matter writing them on a playroom chalkboard or posting them with magnets on a refrigerator door. No, the do's and don'ts for childhood guests in the Woolston household were successfully transmitted via mothering osmosis—via the power of that steely gaze, via sheer maternal authority and presence.

Murle didn't suffer fools lightly—particularly foolish *children*—and was consistently resolute in her dictates and self-assured in her demeanor. Never once did she consult Angie or me as to our "feelings" regarding the Murle Rules. And never once did I witness her waffle or wax and wane on a decision needing to be made. Her yes's were yes and her no's were no.

"No, you may not roll out a double batch of sugar cookie dough on the island counter."

"Yes, you may spend the night, but call your mother first and get her permission."

"No, you may not listen to Disco Duck on Randy's eight-track stereo."

"Yes, you may visit Angie's grandma—but you'd better mind her rules and not drive her crazy!"

Quick and decisive were her actions and rulings. And I liked that, for I always knew where I stood with a mom like Murle. She had a distinctive nonnegotiable way about her which I have come to appreciate and embrace even more over the past two decades of mothering my own three children as well as keeping tabs on a few squirrelly neighborhood kids.

Believe me, for a high-spirited child such as myself, nonnegotiable was a good thing because I took advantage of every inch a mom unwittingly surrendered.

Take soft-spoken Patsy Lybarger, for instance, who ruled with a decidedly different edict than the Power of Murle. Her softer parenting style unwittingly contributed to and encouraged my jumping on her children's beds, eating cereal in her living room, and clandestinely carrying a dead bird into her house and digging through her bedroom closet for a shoe box in which to bury it.* Don't misunderstand; Mrs. Lybarger was a wonderful woman. In fact, I'd nominate Mrs. Lybarger as the sweetest, most thoughtful mom on the entire Buchanan block.

*All verboten at Murle's.

However . . . Mrs. Lybarger thought waaaaaay too highly of me.

See, at Angie's I *knew* Murle was in the house—somewhere—watching, waiting, and (this is key) thinking one or two steps ahead of me. Actually, even when she left physically to go to work and Mr. Woolston was the one puttering in and out keeping parental tabs, it was the intangible presence of *Murle* that kept me (and any prodding pointer fingers) on the straight and narrow.

I always *knew* Murle was the adult and I was the child—she told me that in so many words.

As politically incorrect as it may read, ladies, I feared Murle. And with near-perfect "I'm now the Mom" hindsight, I see how her holding fast to uncompromising authority and guidance ensured both a set standard of behavior in her home and a settled sense of security whenever I was near her.

Boy, have we come—or should I say fallen—a long way

thirty years later. Moms like Murle are in short supply these days, and too many homes find the kids in charge rather than the adult. (Can you say *Supernanny* syndrome?) And it's puzzling, considering all the resources at our disposal:

- Each year thousands of books are published with titles or topics focusing on varying aspects of motherhood.
- Conventions meet featuring the latest, greatest parenting guru with his or her DVDs, CDs, books, study guides, chore charts, rewards charts, potty training charts, and personalized refrigerator magnets—all available at the swipe of a debit card.
- Radio programs feature hosts and guests covering the gamut of mothering subjects, worries, and debate.
- Thirty-two million women seek out parent-driven content online every day while reality shows in all their HDTV glory (perhaps that should read *gory*) feature moms of every social, financial, ethnic, educational, and religious persuasion begging a modern-day Mary Poppins to rescue them from varying forms of deranged offspring.

Motherhood has been sliced and diced, reviewed and dissected every which way.

Yet here's the rub: I find myself writing to and speaking with tens of thousands of women (many of them moms) each year—and I'm struck time and time again by their tales of feeling out of control, ineffective, and more often than not stuck under the embarrassing thumb of a precocious toddler, headstrong preschooler, increasingly mouthy grade-schooler, junior high know-it-all, or hormonally challenged teenager. Sometimes all five.

All those websites.

All those reality shows.

All those books.

All those CDs, DVDs, and ancillary teaching items still being paid off on a credit card.

And yet a certain majority of moms still aren't convinced they know what they're doing when it comes to actually being the mom. Go figure.

I believe this is where I scream at my blinking cursor, call on the Power of Murle, and declare: enough is enough. It's time for a change—better yet, it's time your spawnlings got a dose of long-lasting One Tough Mother change! And here's the best part: there's nothing magical or expensive or elusive about any of it. Honest. The kind of change I'm talking about is fairly simple, really.

No hocus-pocus.

No required four equal payments of $29.95.

No harmful testing on animals. (Well, I suppose that's not completely true; you'll certainly want to test the material presented in this book on any and all wild animals wrecking havoc in your home. But trust me, it won't be harmful in the least. On the contrary, I guarantee it will be one of the most beneficial things you will ever do for yourself and your children.)

See, you don't have to go through your days, weeks, months, and (before you know it) years feeling as though you're anything but confident and in charge. You don't have to feel your life is worthy of a British *Nanny 911** feature

*There is something strangely authoritative sounding about that accent, isn't there? Tell you what—for the remainder of the day (or night), speak to your children with said inflectional dialect and see what happens. If nothing else, it'll be good for a laugh or two.

film (as if an hour program could fix all your "issues"!) or sit around waiting for someone other than you to step up and take the lead.

Ladies, it's not only possible for you to step up and take charge of your kids, it's way past time to do so. That's where this book comes in.

As I've made my way through my own children's developmental stages—infant, toddler, pre-school, adolescence, early young adulthood—I've figured out what can't be put off, undermined, or denied. I've discovered what is absolutely, positively, without apology necessary. And I've become convinced of the nonnegotiables I'm about to present you in the pages of this book.

Now before we go any further, just a word about that term: *nonnegotiable*. The word is pregnant with manipulative possibilities, so let me assure you of what I'm *not* saying and *not* implying with its use. I'm *not* insinuating that you are a lousy mother if you don't embrace each of them. I'm *not* inferring some religious duty to adhere to them. And I'm not suggesting they are the *only* nonnegotiables worthy of One Tough Mother consideration. I *am* boldly suggesting that it takes courage and fortitude to do the work of One Tough Mother. And that the ten vitally important nonnegotiables presented in the following chapters will help align good intention with something even better: decisive action.

You *can* embrace the Power of Murle, have a settled confidence, and step up to be the mom—holding fast your ground and steadily creating a self-assured and authoritative presence in the life of your child. Let's get started, shall we?

# 2

# First Things First

## One Tough Mother Basics

Before we dive into the ten nonnegotiables I mentioned in the last chapter, let me introduce you to what I consider to be the top three qualities or characteristics of One Tough Mother. They're not the Ten Commandments, mind you, set in stone and unable to be edited. Rather, they are a broad summation of sensible, wise, and relevant starting points from my own quest for One Tough Mother confidence these past twenty years.

Some you'll already have under your belt as a mom. Others will seem all but impossible. But all of them— built one upon the other—are guaranteed to strengthen your backbone, undergird your confidence, and shape your character to make you into the One Tough Mother your kids need.

So put your feet up, settle back in your favorite reading spot, and relax. This isn't a test. There's no pass or fail. It's simply you and me purposefully considering powerful under-lying qualities that equip us to become One Tough Mother.

## One Tough Mother Resolutely Knows What's Important

Okay, be honest—am I totally freaking you out with a seeming call to something you can't achieve? It's certainly not my intention. Look, I'm not here to impose some set of impossible-to-meet standards of behavior or actions upon you. Nor am I asking you to compile a nauseatingly long list of One Tough Mother resolutions resembling, as it were, the past ten New Year's resolutions lists you've created and summarily broken or ignored.

I really meant it when I said to relax.

You can breathe in and out knowing I simply want to get your mind on the right track and help you consider the many nuanced dimensions of being One Tough Mother. And this particular one regarding resolutely knowing what is important is, well, of foremost importance.

Now I know this isn't a completely foreign concept to you. After all, you're a mom; determination and firmness are part of your maternal DNA construct, right? And that's exactly what it means to be resolute: to determinedly and firmly make your way toward an end goal.

Easy, huh?

Well, for some, yes. For others, well, it seems it *should* come natural to be determined, firm, and resolute. And many of us thought we *were* determined, firm, and resolute. At least we thought so until we had children—or one child in particular. That's about the time all three flew in the face of our discombobulated reality and it was all over except the British nanny swooping in to save our sorry hide.

Been there? I sure have.

At the ripe old age of twenty-three, my goal was to be a perfect mom. (I like to start out small with something attainable.) Granted, I never actually said, "I am going to be a perfect mom," but in my skewed, young, "how hard can it be" world of zero mothering experience, I thought it . . . and worse still, I believed it was possible.

Mothering Kristen, my firstborn, only encouraged such clueless belief. You see, it seemed to me at the time that I had given birth to a near angel. My days and nights with her were filled with a deep sense of rest, settledness, and *seeming* control, much like the tenderness and love conveyed in an eighteenth-century impressionistic painting by Mary Cassatt.* Granted, Kristen *was* my only child, and that allowed me time to feel rested and settled in my mothering, but at the time I just chalked it up to her and me being more or less perfect.

*You can check out my ideal of "perfect" at www.art. com.

Sigh. Well, perfect lasted until I forgot to take one peach pill (Day 14, if memory serves correctly) of an Ortho-Novum pack, thereby preparing the way for baby number two.

Ricky Neal entered the world eighteen months and nine days after his sister. His healthy birth stats (9 pounds 8 ounces; 22 inches) were matched with an equally healthy set of lungs and appetite for attention. He wasn't colicky a bit. In fact, he was one of the most pleasant little guys you'd ever have the privilege to birth and raise. But he was voracious. And trust me, voracious can do a real number on the goal of being perfect as a mom.

See, when Kristen awoke during the night, I could simply pick her up, change her diaper, settle into a rocker, give her a bottle, and keep my eyes looking straight ahead (as to not encourage her wakefulness). She would half-heartedly drink the bottle's contents until falling back into dreamland.

Kristen just wanted you to take care of what needed tending and let her go back to the job of sleeping. (She's still pretty much like that.) It took all of twenty-two minutes, start to finish, and then we were both down for another good four to six hours of peaceful rest.

Perfect.

But Ricky Neal was an entirely different story. When Ricky Neal woke up, he *really* woke up: eyes open wide, body twisting to and fro, cooing and babbling as he grew a bit older, all in an effort to absorb anything and everything going on around him. (Naturally, this was his routine whether awakening from a late-afternoon nap or at 3:04 a.m. six nights out of the week.)

During those graveyard shifts I would attempt to get in and get out as quickly as possible.

He had other plans.

He wiggled and cooed the moment I picked him up.

He wiggled and cooed and drew me in with devastatingly adorable chocolate brown eyes as I attempted to matter-of-factly change his diaper. (He also peed on me six out of ten times despite valiant "Duck, Cover, and Velcro!" efforts.)

He attacked his bottled meal with gusto, warranting my audible thanks for opting out of breast-feeding.

And as for me keeping my gaze fixed straight ahead? Yeah, like that was going to happen! I am chuckling out loud just writing the memory—this high-spirited, packed to the XY chromosome with gusto baby boy of mine refused to allow such a thing. Between his physical movements, hearty feeding noises, and powerful personality, I was nothing but putty in his hands.

Ricky Neal wanted *alllll* of me. (I've since affectionately referred to him as the child who sucked the life out of me.) And I gave it. First because I loved him; second because I was, after all, aiming for perfect mom status.

It dawned on me around Ricky Neal's six-month birthday that I wasn't cut out to be perfect. (Neither were my children.)

I was tired. I was cranky. I was . . . um, human.

So I opted for "good enough" instead. And while there's certainly nothing morally reprehensible about "good enough," it seemed to be a rather hit-and-miss approach to being a mom.

Flying by the seat of my pants was all it was, really. And when all was said and done, I found it thoroughly unsatisfying. They say a picture paints a thousand words, right? Well, imagine a little Pablo Picasso during his cubism period—that's how I pictured life with Ricky Neal at this particular junction.

Not quite the warm, fuzzy, maternal undertones I had felt with Kristen's arrival, eh?

Life had indeed taken on a decidedly different feel, which led to my eventually asking aloud one day, "Julie, in the light of eternity, what do you want out of this whole mothering thing?" (Translation: Why am I doing this?)

Was perfection truly my end goal?

Or was the goal simply to be a better mom than my sisters-in-law? (Oh, come on! You know you've thought the same type of thing.)

Seriously, what did I want to have accomplished as a mom by the end of my day, month, year, and lifetime? I thought on these things for quite a while, actually, and eventually summed it up with these words: *In the light of eternity, I want to raise children who will want to return home as adults.* (Return as in visit. Not live indefinitely.)

That was it. And given my propensity for talking too much and overstating my case, I captured it quite succinctly at that. Asking The Question naturally led to my determining what truly mattered when it came to the job of mothering. Asking The Question then challenged me to move forward in a firm and resolute fashion in order to accomplish what is truly important to me as a mom.

Hear me on this. If I were writing these words to you as a mother of three children ages ten and under, well, I don't think my words would count for much. Not that any and all mothers with children under age ten *don't* have something to say! Please, please, refrain from sending any hacked off emails to me or my publisher at this point. *I'm just sayin'* . . . it seems I wouldn't really have much "been there" wisdom with which to encourage you, nor could I bear witness to the success or failure of said eternity goal-setting.

But I have been there. And while more challenges certainly lay ahead, this I know as I write to you today: only minutes ago my college freshman daughter laid across my lap as I scratched her back and she sighed and said, "I love our house. I love coming back home to you and Dad." She also hugged me and said, "I'm really glad you're on my side, Mom."

You have no idea how good it felt to hear her words.

I'll go into a bit more detail about *why* that meant so much in a later chapter, but as for here on this page of *One Tough Mother*, suffice it to say her unprompted comments made everything worth it.

Every firm and painful stance I had to take with and sometimes against her: worth it.

Every determined conversation I engaged in and sometimes disengaged from: worth it.

Every major and minor decision I had time to agonize over or was forced to make at the flip of a switch: worth it.

Every prayer I screamed out while driving alone in my van—*God! Help me figure out this child before I . . .* : worth it.

Knowing what mattered and focusing on the big picture changed my mothering perspective.

So let me ask you to take the next few minutes, hours, days, or even weeks to answer The Question: why are you doing what you're doing, and what do you want out of this entire mothering thing? Go ahead, you incredible One Tough Mother wannabe, you! Think it through and answer honestly and candidly concerning what's really important to you about being a mom. Because that's where it all starts.

## One Tough Mother Knows She's Not God

Look, it's not like I ever believed I actually *was* God.

I never claimed to possess some sort of über-spiritual power, nor purported to see or hear questionable revelations from beyond. I simply came to believe what a lot of well-intentioned moms believe: namely, that I should somehow *know where my kids are* 99.9 percent of time; somehow *know what they're doing* 99.9 percent of the time; and somehow *take care of their every need* 99.9 percent of the time. All I was shooting for was

a little infinite awareness (if you're God it's called being omniscient),

mixed with the ability to be present in all places at all times (if you're God it's called being omnipresent),

and a little all-encompassing power thrown in for good measure (and yes, if you're God that's referred to as being omnipotent).

Okay, so it would appear my theological thinking was a bit off-kilter. But I'd be surprised to learn I was the only mother who managed to get her duties twisted with the divine. And I'm saddened by the lack of material addressing this matter in basic mothering manuals. Oh, plenty of discussion is paid to control freak matters, but discourse regarding the spiritual issue underlying it all . . . eh, not so much.

I've always found this to be frustrating and a bit disconcerting. After all, interest in faith and spiritual belief seems to ratchet up with each passing year. *Newsweek* and *Time* magazines highlight matters of faith numerous times a year. And while some may argue that these journalistic endeavors present positions far removed from traditionally held Judeo-Christian tenets, the mere fact that America's top news magazines are paying attention to people's pursuit of spirituality is telling, to say the least.

And yet spirituality alone is never enough for the long haul of dealing with life in the day-to-day matters of raising, protecting, and teaching children and even less so when it comes to far weightier matters of the eternal. Popular spirituality extols an individual's choice to figure out what "works" when it comes to life and eternity. Popular spirituality looks inward more than upward and subtly convinces us that believing in a general sense of "god-ness" or something bigger than one's own self is enough. But therein lies the "won't cut it" rub: you see, mere spirituality isn't relationship—and relationship is what we so desperately need as mothers and as women. One Tough Mother (book and author) unapologetically presupposes, supports, and proclaims the divine reality of God over mere spirituality, joyfully asserting the divine reality of a loving God who delights (yes! delights!) in naturally and gloriously intersecting our lives with his truth, his love, and his power.

Listen, I'll have celebrated my forty-second birthday by the time you read these pages, and I can tell you based on personal experience and confidences shared by thousands of mothers that vague spirituality can and will take you only so far. There will come a time (mark it down) in each of our lives as mothers when we are forced to cry "Uncle!" to matters anchored to hollow religion, mere spirituality, or our own frailty and anything-but-divine-anythingness.

My husband once likened me to the persistent terrier who yipped about Spike the Bulldog's paws in the old Warner Brothers cartoons. Over and over again, the canine squirt would bounce around Spike, asking time and time again, "Can I go with you, Spike? Huh? Can I, can I, can I, can I go, Spike?"*

"You're just like that," Rick said. "When you get an idea in your head or have a conviction about something, you're relentless. You don't give up. You will outlast anyone and everyone and not quit until you've finished what you started."

I still consider it one of the finest compliments he's ever paid me.

Yet all that tenacity fell to the wayside several years into motherhood. For countless days (weeks, even) I was worn down and wrung out, and at times I looked at one child in particular and longingly thought, "Okay, if I was forced to send one of my children away for a long, long time . . ."

*For similar mothering imagery, picture a persistent toddler poking an upper thigh while repeating "Momma, Momma, Momma, Momma, Momma . . ."

I grew plenty tired, plenty of times, but two specific times perfectly highlight the impoverished worth of anything I could actually do by my own power.

You see, when you're standing helplessly by watching paramedics work on your eight-week-old son—his breath ragged and asthmatic—spirituality doesn't cut it. Your mind and your heart and your soul scream for the One who *can* help those trying to help your baby breathe, because you have come to the awful realization there is nothing *you* can do.

When your angry teenage child storms out yet again and you are faced with the cold silence of their room, visual remnants of childhood lost, and a stomach threatening to retch—spirituality doesn't cut it. Your mind and your heart and your soul scream for the One who *can* see where they are, the One who knows who they are with, and the

One who longs to thread the loose ends of your family back together again—or give you a knot to hold onto as he works—because you know that *you* are utterly powerless to change the inner workings of your child's heart.

Neither mere spirituality nor religion will help for the long haul, for both are disastrously contingent upon us—mortal, finite, and weariness-prone women. So a relationship of surrender to (and trust in) the One who shores our reserves, grants us the ability to love our children, and hears and answers the most sublime of prayers is the wisest One Tough Mother precept you'll ever choose to follow.

## One Tough Mother Holds On to Her Sexy Self

*This One Tough Mother is unafraid to admit . . .*

I own dozens and dozens of shoes with two-and-a-half-plus-inch heels and only one pair of flats.

My favorite color of clothing is red—bold, rich, "Here I am!" red.

There isn't a diet pill I haven't consumed or seriously considered swallowing.

I've enthusiastically (and unapologetically) gone under the plastic surgery knife.

Spanx tames my thighs, Tweezerman plucks my brows, and an old-school razor blade keeps my legs smooth and sleek.

My toenails are currently painted a deep-hued Malaga Wine shade.

I can testify to the miraculous separating uplift of Victoria's underwire.

*At the same time . . .*

My lids now take 3.6 seconds to "snap" back after an application of eye shadow.
Three new freckles (i.e., sun spots) now dot my right shoulder.
My left knee randomly "pops."
A size ten skirt (which I've owned since 2003) has *never* made it higher than two inches above my knees—this, despite wearing Spanx.
I find myself consciously reminding myself to clinch my thighs together whenever I feel a sneeze or serious belly laugh coming on.
And I no longer pretend I'm going to begin an exercise and weight lifting regime.

*All that to say . . .*

I'm a forty-one-year-old One Tough Mother who believes that one should never, never, never concede defeat when it comes to maintaining and accessorizing "The Package."

Now, hold on! Don't turn the page or put this book down altogether thinking I'm about to go into some carbs vs. calories vs. fad dieting spiel. I am not.

Don't roll your eyes or dismiss this short section believing I'm about to intone some exercise mantra speech regarding how many abdominal crunches you need to do to get back your pre–C-section midriff. (You know what? I believe I will go ahead and answer that one: zero. The operative words in this particular situation are "tummy tuck.")

And please don't allow your feelings to be even slightly stepped on due to a fear I'm going to make you feel bad for not having thought of this matter in the least since having children. Or for the fact that you're still wearing splotches of toenail polish applied sometime around the fall of 2005.

Take a deep breath and relax. I'm not going to do anything of the kind. This is simply a short and sassy shout-out to those who feel they have lost or set aside their feminine, sexy selves as babies, toddlers, disgustingly lithe teenage daughters, and mothering responsibilities came along and set up house. I know you're out there . . .

Ms. Wearing a Nursing Bra and Your Baby Is Eight Years Old

Ms. Dearfoams *Are* Your Sexy Shoe of Choice

Ms. Spent the Entire Week in Your Sweats with Spit-Up Stains

Ms. Alluring Scent Behind Your Ear Is Peanut Butter

Ms. Lying in Bed and Not Being Touched by a Spouse or Spawnling for a Twenty-Four-Hour Period *Is* My Secret Fantasy

Ms. Only Uses Tweezers to Pick a Tick Off a Kid's Head

Ms. Can't Get Over the Fact Your Stomach Rests on Your Upper Thighs

Ms. Feels Guilty for Spending Money on Coloring Your Hair When the Kids So Desperately Need *One More* PlayStation Game

Ms. I Would if I Could . . . On Second Thought, *Nahhh*

*If you don't believe me, check out the appendix of this book. The options are a little mind-boggling, but if you choose wisely, time and money spent maintaining and accessorizing "the Package" is worth it!

I know you're there, and I've felt your pain and shared your fantasy!

"The Package" requires time and money and more time and more money to maintain.*

What used to sit up and say "Hello!" sans support

now requires an engineering contraption worthy of the National Medal of Technology. Calves avalanche and produce cankles. Hair falls from your head and appears in your nostrils.

Feet flatten.

Derrieres widen.

Shoulders broaden.

But in all these things we are more than conquerors! Seriously, girls, I believe it's so important to keep on keeping on when it comes to feeling beautiful and looking attractive. And you know why? Because you and I were girls—women—long before we were mothers.

I mean, let's be One Tough Mother real with one another here. I'm not some simpering female who can't leave the house without her eyeliner on, mind you, and I'm certainly not asking you to become one either. I just don't want us to ever think it's okay to throw in the towel, hit the couch, eat Fritos, and watch marathon sessions of the Lifetime Movie Network programming just because we've had children, we've become mothers, and our bodies are no longer as taut, firm, and supple as they were X amount of months and years ago.

It's not about being the prettiest girl in the room, town, or cosmos. It's not about having the tightest abs or the fullest lips. It's about *you* being comfortable in *your* skin and enjoying every moment—okay, let's try for a more realistic 83.5 percent of the moments—you're in it.

So throw away those ridiculous "look how thin I was in high school" photos you pull out every third year or so to compare yourself against. News flash! There's a 99.9 percent chance your body will never look like that again in your life no matter how many meals you skip, how many miles you tread, or how many "procedures" you consider. And who wants to look (and act and feel about themselves) like they did way back then anyway? I mean, come on!

Just this past summer, I finally threw away my high school senior memory book. It was loaded with memories I didn't necessarily want to remember (or have my children read) and photo after photo of size 10 Calvin Klein me. I thought I was huge at the time (of course) and over the years had trekked up the attic stairs on more than one occasion when I felt overweight and ugly and just wanted to make myself a bit more depressed.

Then, *boom*! I looked at myself one day and I thought, "Forget this mess. I'm a grown woman with grown woman hips and grown woman breasts and grown woman laugh lines—I like the skin I'm in." And that was that. I tossed the book out with the trash and never thought twice about it.

If you've got a similar set of "back in the day" images that are hindering your ability to reasonably and appropriately maintain and love the skin you're in today, it's time for you to toss 'em too. Enough of being held hostage to a particular dress size, image, or memory of whatever. It's One Tough Mother time to step up and choose to live in the present, shed the past, and let go of unrealistic fantasies of being (and looking like) someone you're not.

Once you do that tossing, you'll be ready to find that misplaced sexiness of yours and reclaim your confidence as an attractive woman—confidence that can't help but spill over into your role as One Tough Mother.

So there you have it. The foundation for your One Tough Mother status: Know what's important. Let God be God and hold off on taking the divine reins! And make it a priority to hold on to that sexy self of yours.

Get those building blocks in place, and you'll be ready for the heart of this book—for the ten nonnegotiable principles that will transform you fully from one tired and tenuous mother to One Tough Mother.

# 3

# Sit Down and Shut Up

## Nonnegotiable #1:
## Be the Boss (without Apology!)

Oh, dear. I've lost some of you already, haven't I?

You're sitting there reading the page wondering why I would commit *the* sure-sign-of-a-bad-mom phrase to chapter title print when perfectly good euphemisms would suffice:

"Sit down and zip it."

"Sit down and clam up."

"Sit down and can it."

"Sit down and tone it down."

"Sit down and stifle."

"Sit down and close your mouth."

"Sit down and be quiet."

"Sit down and hush."

"Sit down and sssshhhh . . ."

"Sit down and don't say another word."

Why not use one of those, you may be wondering?

Simple. I'd like you to regard me as an *honest mom and author* as much as a mothering expert, and for better or worse this very real mom has hurled the double *S* phrase on more than one occasion.

Waaay more.

Oh, don't get me wrong—I fought the urge to do so. I promised before ever having children that I would hold myself to a higher verbal standard. My words would be governed with firm kindness, sweetness, and infinite patience. I would never shriek my way through motherhood like the woman I had observed as a fifteen-year-old girl scarfing down a meal at Pizza Hut with my friends.

*Good grief,* I thought back then, *how hard can it possibly be to be the mom? And what lame excuse for a mom resorts to bellowing "Shut up!" at her kids, especially in public?*

Then . . . as the saying goes . . . I went to college, fell in love, got married, ineffectively used birth control (twice!), had children, and found myself pushing a shopping cart through Martin's Grocery Store in 1993.

Basic food items (monstrous cans of Juicy Juice, a family-size box of Cheerios, various fresh fruit, and boxes of Kraft macaroni and cheese) were stacked on top of my purse while my four-and-a-half-year-old daughter and three-year-old son stood (yes, I know you're not supposed to let them do that) in the cart belting out the grating lyrical refrain, "Mommy you big fat doo-doo! Mommy you big fat doo-doo!"

Lovely.

I could have let the doo-doo comment slide (there's a critical brain-numbing fatigue you get after X number of hours listening to such stuff), but big fat? Um, I don't think so. They continued on with their sorry little sibling duet, over and over, despite my protests and telling them to "Sit down and zip it!" Louder and louder they sang, drawing the attention of a pimple-faced shelf stocker and an irritated dairy manager, so I chose what I believed to be an excellent "Be the boss" tactic: lowering my voice, sticking my pointer finger a quarter inch from their foreheads, and menacingly commanding, "Sit down and don't say another word."

Instead, they looked at one another, burst out laughing, and with *Children of the Corn* synchronicity robustly shouted, "Doo-doo, Mommy!" (What *is* it with toddlers and senseless insults?)

About that time Ricky Neal decided to biff a couple of grapes off my forehead, which sent Kristen reeling in convulsive giggles. And that, my friend, is *exactly* when my left eyelid began to twitch, my lower jaw clenched, and I hurled it. With spittle punctuating every staccato word, I ripped and roared for customer and produce manager alike to hear, "Both of you sit down and *shuddddup!*"

And guess what?

They sat down and . . .

zipped it,

clammed up,

canned it,

toned it down,

stifled,

closed their mouths,

fell quiet,

hushed,

sssshhhhed,

and didn't say another word.

"Be the boss" mission accomplished, right? Or was it?

Both kids stood in stunned (glorious) silence for approximately fourteen seconds until Kristen leaned toward her brother, whispered conspiratorially in his ear, leveled her gaze, and then pronounced gravely, "Ricky, Mommy gots a potty mouth."

A moment passed and both children, realizing what she had just said, squealed with glee and began chanting even louder than before, "Mommy gots potty mouth! Mommy gots potty mouth! Mommy gots . . ." Oh, boy.

Ever pushed a grocery cart a mile in my shoes? Or chastised yourself for doing such a brilliant job teaching your children inappropriate word usage?

You're certainly not alone, trust me. Not too long ago an older friend of mine shared with me the following story about her two-year-old granddaughter and twenty-seven-year-old daughter.

It seems my friend's daughter had allowed her child to stand in a grocery cart (this is why we're not supposed to do it, ladies), and as she reached left to pick up a box of Chex cereal, the two-year-old reached right for the Pop-Tarts. Unfortunately, she reached a bit too far and—just before her mother could catch her—fell onto the cold concrete floor, landing on her right arm.

The toddler began to cry, and the young mother immediately suspected a broken or severely sprained arm. Leaving the contents of her cart, she made her way out of the store, called and requested an emergency office visit with her family physician, and made her way to the doctor's office. Sure enough, after careful examination and a quick X-ray, a hairline fracture was confirmed, and the doctor's orders were to put the daughter's arm in a soft cast and rest it in the supportive confines of a sling. All the details were taken care of, and mother and daughter left none too worse for wear.

You know where this is going, don't you?

Sure enough, my friend called her daughter less than twenty-three hours after the cast and sling were prescribed and asked how things were going. "Not so great," her daughter replied. "Jessica isn't wearing her sling." Why not, her mother asked, was something wrong? Had she injured it further since returning home? "No," said her daughter with a defeated sigh, "Jessica just doesn't want to use it."

*Huh?* Three questions and three observations. I promise I'll be brief.

1. How old is little Miss Jessica? (Ah, yes, two years old.)
2. How old is little Miss Jessica's mom? (Aha! Twenty-seven years old.)
3. Who's the boss? (Miss Jessica is the leading contender!)

# Wimpy Moms

Motherhood is not for the faint of heart. A two-year-old can and will chew you up and spit you back out with the ease of chewing gum. And older kids, well, they are beyond brutal. That's why someone has to be in charge. Someone has to stand up in the chaotic world of family and declare in so many words—methinks these exact words, perhaps—"I'm the boss."

Think I'm being too harsh or overstating my case? If so, consider the following news excerpt regarding a story that broke in early January 2007. Read it and ask yourself, "What would One Tough Mother have done?"

At a high school in McKinney, Texas, officials say a group of five cheerleaders recently got out of control. Dubbed the

"Fab Five," they acted like they could get away with almost anything and refused to bend to authority. They repeatedly skipped class, insulted their instructors, and terrorized their coach, their fourth coach in just one year. . . . *Some are pointing fingers at the mother of the clique's ringleader, who was also the school's principal* [emphasis mine]. . . . "This culture developed where the principal's daughter and her friends were above consequences," said attorney Harold Jones, who was hired by the school district to look into complaints about the cheerleaders. In December, the principal resigned as part of a settlement in which she received $75,000 and a letter of recommendation for her next job. The former principal's attorney says she denies shielding her daughter from punishment. But Jones says it wasn't just the principal who was at fault, but an entire school administration and parents who didn't enforce the rules are to blame. "Kids are going to be kids. They're going to figure out ways to push your limits," Jones said. "Adults have to be adults."[1]

Raise your hand if you'd prefer *not* to have your name plastered all over the news media making you the official pinup for Inept Wimpy Moms everywhere. This isn't brain surgery—be the adult, indeed. This story alone should drive us to the bookshelves to purchase scads and scads of *One Tough Mother* for all the less-than-authoritative mothers we may know.

## And You Are . . . ?

Someone has to be the boss, and if you are a card-carrying member of the motherhood race, well, guess what—you're it. Now, some of us came by this being the boss thing quite naturally. We've never had to think twice about barking out orders and asserting our presence with our own children—or those of complete strangers. Others . . . well, it just doesn't come so natural. And I'll tell you where you can see this reality played out better than anywhere—at any local store near you.

I'm going to let you in on something I've done for years now. Whenever I'm shopping—be it at the grocery store, at my local Target, or cruising through the aisles of Sephora—my eyes are always on the lookout for any and all wigged-out moms and their equally wigged-out children. Maybe you've run into a few of these yourself.

### Ambivalent Mom

Poor thing. I go absolutely crazy watching her go back and forth . . . not quite certain . . . unable to decide what course of action to take.

*Enter Ambivalent Mom*: "Should I make my eight-year-old quit trying to shove his five-year-old sister underneath the cart or just keep saying, 'Stop it now, that's not nice'?"

Hmmm, what to do? What to do?

### Expletive Mom

Oh, come on, we've all heard her spewing a blue streak over teeming Shop-Mart masses at some point in time. You can't have an honest One Tough Mother list without her. It goes something like this:

*Enter Expletive Mom*: "I told you to put down that *#$@! package of Skittles ten minutes ago, now take the #($!&^ candy and put it back on the %$&^ counter where it belongs before I . . ."

Well, you get the idea: lots of colorful language and a whole lot of nothing when it comes to positively influencing her children's public behavior.

### Oblivious Mom

Everyone *but* Oblivious Mom sees and hears and feels motivated to do something about her children. Perhaps it's her rowdy teenagers whom she needs to instruct to tone down their raucous voices so as not to overwhelm conversations taking place around them (Rick and I sat next to this family at Red Lobster in 1999). Or it could be a six-year-old who refuses to remain seated for longer than ninety-three seconds and keeps jumping up, climbing under the table, and weaving her way in and around wait staff (I wanted to punt kick this little sprout sometime around May 2005 during an evening out with my girlfriends).

*Enter . . .* um, wait a minute, Oblivious Mom *never* enters the picture.

### Not-Going-to-Tell-You-Again Mom

Okay, quick confession: I have been this mother lots and lots of times. Just wanted you to know.

There you stand—six persons deep in a slow-moving grocery checkout line. Waiting behind you—*directly* behind you—is a family of four. One mom and three, well, I'll refer to them as "Its" for the sake of our discussion.

"It" Number One is picking its nose—intently.

*Enter Not-Going-to-Tell-You-Again Mom*: "I'm not going to tell you again—stop picking your nose in public."

Then you spy another "It" standing behind Mom—maybe three-and-a-half feet tall at the most. It Number Two randomly steps out from behind Mom and grandly waves a well-worn sippy cup back and forth in the air. *It looks too old for a sippy cup*, you think while keeping an observant eye on the increasingly broad hand gestures of nose-picker It.

About that time, It Number Three, who is straining forward in the shopping cart, has had enough of the sippy cup taunting and begins battering its feet against the steel cart, puffs up its face, and lets loose verbal baby bedlam.

*Enter Not-Going-to-Tell-You-Again Mom* (now staring daggers at three-and-a-half-foot It): "I told you before coming in here and again back in toys to stop teasing your baby sister. Now I'm not going to tell you again—give back her sippy cup!"

## Terrorized by a Toddler (or Two) Mom

This was me in that grocery store aisle with Kristen and Ricky Neal. And I'm willing to bet it's been you at times too. Sound familiar? Look familiar?

Oh, we are such a mess sometimes as moms, aren't we?

Let's all just take a deep breath and face that fact and remind ourselves of the most important thing: we're still here and we're still trying. We keep on trying! That's what we have to hold to. Sure, we've been one of those moms I described, but we've kept on keeping on—buying books (such as this one), listening to those we trust, and going to bed and waking up morning after morning and deciding to do it all over again. We may be a mess, but we're here and we're ready to do things a little different or perhaps to establish a presence that until this time has eluded us.

The majority of moms I've met while researching material for *One Tough Mother* told me they want to enjoy being the mom. They also told me they didn't necessarily know how to go about that despite their age, education, and mothering experience thus far in their lives. And I'm not really all that surprised. I was there myself a time or two. I had a bachelor's degree in elementary education but couldn't (still can't) explain why boys love to stick their fingers between their toes and then ask you to smell them. So how on earth was I supposed to know the best ways to set myself up as a strong authority figure in my children's lives?

Has your child ever asked who gets to be your boss? My youngest did so around age seven. The family and I had watched an episode of *Malcolm in the Middle* and were listening to the closing musical score declaring, "You're not the boss of me now, you're not the boss of me now . . ." (I loved Jane Kaczmarek's hilarious no-nonsense portrayal of Lois, much put-upon mother of four boys and wife to one seriously skewed husband.)

Patrick suddenly perked up and I smiled, for I could almost see the wheels turning in his second-grade head. *This should be good*, I thought. Flopping his tan legs over mine, he sighed and then queried, "Mom, who's the Big Boss of you?"

What'd I tell you? Some question, huh?

Smiling even more, I replied, "Well, your daddy, of course."

Well, I thought I was going to have to perform the Heimlich as said daddy laughed aloud and then nearly choked on the post-*Malcolm* sub sandwich he was enjoying.

Truth is, Rick and I have always practiced a more egalitarian style of marriage. It's not as though I don't listen to him or I refuse to do what he may ask, yea, even *tell* me to do on certain occasions. Far from it, actually, as I've learned over the years the wisdom of listening to a man who has known me over half my life, puts up with my sometimes less-than-stellar wifely and motherly ways, and still reports for breakfast every morning. I listen and even (gasp!) obey, but neither Rick nor I would consider him the Big Boss of me.*

*Please send any and all letters of dissent to the care of my publisher.

Patrick noticed the humor sparks between his daddy and me and complained, "Aw, come on, Mom, I'm serious—tell me who really gets to boss you around?" Enjoying the moment, I decided to see what he was thinking (making it one of those teaching moment mom things I've been doing since he was a baby learning how to speak) and chose to toss it back his way: "Well, tell you what, Patrick, why don't *you* tell me who you think it is?"

He thought about it for a short while, looked to his daddy and then back to me, and replied, "Well, Daddy is your boss sometimes, like when he tells you he's going to watch all the *Andy Griffith* he wants even though you don't like it, but I think God is your Big Boss and you have to do what he says all the time."

Smart kid, that Patrick.

Then again, I'd been drilling said truth into his head for years and years.

## Things We Do Instead of Being the Boss

As mentioned in chapter 2, this One Tough Mother author unapologetically presupposes the divine reality of a loving God who delights in intersecting my life and yours with truth, love, power, and (most importantly to the conversation at hand) divine authority. Mind you, this is not some capricious authority tossing mere mortals about with whim or fancy but a resolute, sure, and divine relational authority to which we can tether our lives and parental responsibilities both as women and as mothers.

And we need it, because it never gets any easier being a mom.

I know it's difficult to try to stand your ground day after day and not lose your temper and fleeting sense of control in the process.

I know it's wearing to train and teach your children principles you know they need in order to grow up to become decent men and women.

I know it's challenging for married, single, divorced, teenage, midlife, rich, poor, and middle-class moms to be the boss.

And I know more than any of the above that you can't do it alone—at least not for the long haul—and if your only form of strength is another person or your own ability and will, well, you're going to wear out somewhere down the road. We all need God's strength, and trust me, I know it can be difficult to come to the point of realizing and accepting this truth. I think it goes back to our believing we're somehow supposed to—expected to—figure it all out by ourselves, as though that makes us a better mom, a tougher mom.

But it doesn't work like that. We can't do it alone, and when we make a mess, there's no way we can begin to clean it up or fix it based on our abilities alone. I don't think I'm overstating when I tell you that if I hadn't acknowledged (and conformed to) God's authority in my life, well, I'd probably be writing this from a state prison or long-term mental health facility.

My early years of being an angry, out-of-control mother who crossed the line physically and verbally with her children are well documented in my first book, *She's Gonna Blow: Real Help for Moms Dealing with Anger*. I never set out to abuse the authority I held as mother to Kristen and Ricky Neal, and I never intended to become a poster child for authoritarian whack jobs.

But I did—for a time.

Those first five years were some of the scariest, most shameful, and most powerless times of my life. It was obvious to me that what I was doing wasn't working, but more importantly, what I *believed* regarding parental authority and training my children was neither effective nor healthy for my children's physical, mental, or spiritual well-being.

Truth be told, I was way off base as a twentysomething mother of two children under age four. I wrongfully equated being louder than my kids with being the boss; wrongfully equated controlling my kids in public with being the boss; wrongfully equated "Sit down and shut up!" with "Be the boss" power; and wrongfully assumed just being the mom, period, would somehow translate into knowing what to do and how to do it well.

I had to make my way out of a lot of immature and ineffective behavior and discover practical, doable truth regarding what it really means to take the lead and be the mom. Within days of the Sit Down and Shut Up Incident of '93, I began paying closer attention to the things I said, the behavior I demonstrated, and the overall beliefs I had regarding motherhood. I started noting what worked and what failed miserably because I wanted to bring about some of the "in the light of eternity" goals I mentioned in chapter 2—even though I didn't necessarily know at the time that that's what I was doing. And one thing that was clear was that I needed to get a handle on this being the boss stuff. I started learning then—and have been working on it ever since.

Just this last winter I had been working on the manuscript for *One Tough Mother* and was having trouble with this chapter in particular (translation: I had been sitting at the computer hour after hour bashing my head against the keyboard and wailing). I had read through all my notes, read through parenting books, scoured the Internet, and called up numerous friends in hopes of hitting inspirational gold while talking with them.

But I kept coming up with nothing.

Then, after what seemed days and days of nothing, I remembered an audio teaching series I had purchased and listened to from Dr. James MacDonald titled *Family Revival: God's Wisdom at My House.*\* Eureka! I recalled Dr. MacDonald's points about parents training their children in truth, in which he aptly identifies similar mistakes we make in failing to step up to the task of being the boss. Looking back, I can identify how I made each of them in my early years of mothering. See if one or more resonate with your experience too.

\*I encourage you to purchase your own set of CDs for the series at www.walkintheword.org.

Instead of owning "be the boss" authority, some mothers choose to:

abdicate: not show up
delegate: leave it up to someone else
relegate: put off to different time, year, place, child[2]

Food for thought, huh? Let's look at each one.

### Give It Up

Perhaps you, like me, associated that first action with royalty—you may recall learning in history class about the historical scandal of December 10, 1936, when King Edward VIII abdicated his right to sit on the throne as King of England. (Okay, so maybe you *don't* remember that. Trust me, it happened.) Can you imagine giving up rule of an entire country—overthrowing centuries of pomp and circumstance and obligation? It was breathtaking and heart-wrenching in historical and personal scope, but it was no greater than the abdication of power, responsibility, obligation, and duty some of us have willfully chosen as mothers. And I suspect the weight of our abdication lies as heavy on the heart of God as that of an actual King of England.

Fact is, some moms simply never show up for the job of being the boss. They prefer, perhaps, the role of friend to that of parental authority figure. They are AWOL when it comes to the active tense responsibilities of establishing rules, boundaries, and expectations and then following through. I've often wondered, "Can one *subconsciously* abdicate authority?" Is it possible to wake up one morning, look at your children, and *not* know when you relinquished your place of authority in their life?

I've yet to figure out the answer. Part of me can't help but consider how abdication relates to our individual temperaments and mothering styles. For example, I am an all-or-nothing extrovert who doesn't know how to do anything halfway. I've never been able to "fly under the radar" in any way whatsoever. What you see and hear is what you get. I rarely decide anything without having first wrestled with very deep feelings about the matter. Quite frankly, I wear myself out—and probably my family as well. So abdicating my authority as a mother (which I have done at times) occurred only after I'd put an extraordinary degree of forethought into the choice.

But that's just me.

Your basic personality, mothering style, and way of dealing (or not) with duty, obligation, and responsibility may run in a completely opposite direction. I guess the most important factor in the entire discussion is this: we all need to avoid at all costs abdicating any of those mothering imperatives—for there is an unimaginable consequence involved in doing so. Consider the wording of the Instrument of Abdication which King Edward VIII signed that December morning in 1936:

I, Edward the Eighth, of Great Britain, Ireland, and the British Dominions beyond the Seas, King, Emperor of India, do hereby declare My irrevocable determination to renounce the Throne for Myself and for My descendants.[3]

I literally caught my breath upon reading *"and for My descendants."* What a cost for abdication! Dare I propose such selfishness also? Our willful choice to abdicate our "be the boss" responsibilities and leadership will come at a cost and be a loss for our children. There's no way around it—if we don't show up, moms, our children will bear the brunt.

### *Hand It Over*

The second crutch we often go to when abstaining from being the boss is delegating responsibilities to someone else entirely. Now, I'm going to go out on a limb, so be merciful if the branch breaks and you see me hurtling headlong to the hard ground below. At the very least, cover my body before you leave. Here goes: I think moms (and Christian moms in particular) try to justify this particular action more than any other listed. I don't have any qualms making such an observation because

1. I'm a Christian,
2. I'm a mom,
3. I've delegated responsibilities which were mine to take, and
4. I've seriously tried to justify having done so.

Most of us have enough sense to recognize that someone has to be acting as an authority figure in our child's life. Here's how I think it works for many of us. We know it's in our children's best interests and even recognize the spiritual need for and nature of our being the boss and establishing the necessary spiritual structure and guidelines both we and our children need.

So we do just that—we dive in with child number one with all the gusto we can manage. Depending on our personality, ambitious nature, and perception of what is most needed, we get to it—but in the process we grow weary. Perhaps we add another child or two or three to the family unit. Or we find ourselves juggling more work responsibilities with our time at home. It could be due to a hundred and one varying factors, but eventually we grow weary—we're spent—and bit by bit we find ourselves choosing to disengage from the role of being the boss.

If we are Christian moms, we probably have a healthy (and in all likelihood God-given) sense of conviction telling us something isn't right. We're needled by our lack of interest or avoidance, so we do what good Christian moms do: we attempt to supplement and make up the difference with someone or something else. We

sign them up for Vacation Bible School,

enroll them in Christian education,

get friendly with the youth leaders and pay for our teen to attend Winter Snow Blast III,

buy VeggieTales DVDs,

play Bible songs on CD, and even, perhaps,

send them to Grandma and Grandpa's for a while and hope they do and say things that make up for where you're lacking.

Oh, my, I have most definitely been there.

It was late 1998 and my year had consisted of managing homeschool teaching plans for second and fourth grade; taking care of Patrick as he slowly (over an eighteen-month period) grew out of apnea events, reoccurring bouts of asthma, and upper respiratory illnesses warranting hospitalization; weathering severe financial problems; and dipping my toes (or perhaps that should read "lips") in the waters of public speaking.

The previous year I had been gung-ho regarding being the boss of my children and had enthusiastically taught the older children a Bible class, encouraged them to memorize simple Bible verses, and even purchased a rather intimidating "Christian catechism" manual to ensure they learned precepts of the Judeo-Christian faith. (It would seem my all-or-nothing mode of living extends to the classroom as well.)

Thirteen months later I was happy just to get through core classes of reading, math, and social studies. I was worn out and decided to relegate some of the spiritual aspects of mothering to the lovely members of my church in Galesburg, Illinois. Each Wednesday I happily "dumped" the two older children for Awana classes, left Patrick in the nursery, and then drove away and scoured the endcaps at Target looking for marked-down housewares.

Now, am I saying it's a mortal sin to take your kids to church classes and leave? Certainly not! However, when we are doing so as part of delegating core responsibilities of being the boss—well, I'm thinking that may not fly so much.

We do the above and find a multitude of other ways to delegate spiritual authority, all in hopes of our children "catching" good teaching and strong examples and somehow managing to grow up to be kids who don't embarrass us. Sigh. Of course, all of those substitutes are better than nothing. But let's be realistic here: the single most important person and model of character to your children is you.

You must show up as guide and guardian.

You must train your children in honesty.

You must know who they're hanging out with and what they're thinking about life.

You must establish the rules and guidelines—and then incorporate them into the day-to-day routine of your wonderfully ordinary life with your kids.

You must be the boss and take the lead.

## Put It Off

Perhaps you neither abdicate nor delegate. Where might you fall in shirking One Tough Mother status?

It may be in relegating your "be the boss" responsibilities to a different time or different child. Dr. MacDonald spoke of the parent who says, "Oh, I agree with you, but my child is only seven years old. . . . I'll do the things I need to do when he's a little older." I've thought of the mother who looks at her children and decides to put off "being the boss" until her oldest can understand more, or until her youngest isn't nursing or teething or potty training or experiencing night terrors, or until all her children can get in and out of a car seat without help.

Wisdom says otherwise. If we would pour as much as possible as soon as possible into our child, we'd never live to regret it. You and I both know there will always—forever and always—be some reason to put off till tomorrow what needs to be done today.

Julie, I would take more care to be the boss in my child's life, but it seems like my life is one life crisis after another—I just can't do it.

Julie, I would take more care to be the boss consistently in my child's life, but the day-to-day responsibilities of working and taking care of the house and planning the children's school schedules leave me drained—I just can't do it.

Julie, if I wasn't so physically tired from all I do . . .

Julie, if money wasn't such an issue . . .

Sound familiar?

I've already admitted as much for myself.

There will always be circumstances that can become excuses for not being the boss or putting off what needs to be said and done today. Circumstances that can and will lead to our final inaction regarding being the boss.

But don't do it! Don't relegate "be the boss" wisdom and leadership to a tomorrow we don't even know will ever arrive or to the tiresome realities of today.

## Stepping Up

Look, we've probably all shifted the priority of being the boss and used one of the above as a reason at some time or another as a mother. But think back to the question I posed several pages ago: is it possible to abdicate, delegate, or relegate our "be the boss" responsibilities without knowing it?

The more I consider my own words, the less apt I am to believe so. We may not understand all the varying factors at play. But we do, at some point, consciously choose to turn away.

We choose to abdicate.

We choose to delegate.

We choose to relegate.

I hope you haven't read this far and said, "You know, so far nothing she has written about pertains to me." You're probably getting a lot more out of this if you're able to say, "Man! I never realized that's what I was doing or thinking." The important thing is recognizing the basic principles of One Tough Mother truth that will equip you to do things differently and successfully.

You don't have to continue doing tomorrow what you did today or yesterday.

You can find your backbone, step up, and be the boss!

You can choose to rescind your abdication and take back your rightful throne.

You can choose to cut back the voices speaking into your children's lives and project yours first and foremost.

You can kick responsibility back upstairs where it belongs—with you.

Now, if you're anything like me, that all sounds fine and dandy, but some practical examples, thoughts, and suggestions would make it that much better. Say no more—I've compiled a list just for you. Read it through and consider which ones fit your personality as a mom and the dynamics of your children and family.

Pick one tactic and stick with it for longer than an hour, a day, or even a week. Stick with it until it becomes a habit (usually a minimum of twenty-one days, by the way). And feel free to put a little of this with a little of that and see what works best for you. The main thing is to keep trying to build your "be the boss" authority and confidence within the family ranks.

### Speak Truth

Patrick is my youngest child, but for some reason his warped little brain believes otherwise. I think I know why. There's nearly a seven-year age gap between him and his brother and sister. As a result he has grown up quickly (taking certain cues from them both) and on occasion adopted a certain air of, shall we say, bravado that neither his brother nor sister had the nerve to attempt.

He's always been an agreeable child but became somewhat argumentative in early grade school. One day in particular stands out, from when he was around seven years of age. I can't begin to recall the topic at hand, but our conversation ended with the following dialogue that he had heard verbatim between his brother and sister and me many times over the years. He knew both my lines and his well enough (no cues were needed), and it went exactly like this:

> ME: "Patrick, who's the boss?"
>
> PATRICK: "You are." (He says dejectedly.)
>
> ME: "Patrick, who's going to win?"
>
> PATRICK: "You are." (He says with resignation.)
>
> ME: "Patrick, why am I going to win?"
>
> PATRICK: "Because you're the boss." (And sighs gloomily.)

Never let them see you sweat—that's what I've been telling myself since the at-home pregnancy stick turned blue in 1988. And the above dialogue is just one simple way you can begin implementing "be the boss" firmness in your home with your children. Do so with a light but firm tone of voice. Let them see a twinkle in your eye, but maintain a composure that communicates you mean business.

I tried never to bully the children with this conversational dialogue. At times my implementing the first question would have been inappropriate and a bit thoughtless. Other times I knew the children were tuning me out so completely that it would only encourage them in their crabbiness and, yes, even belligerence. So I kept my mouth closed.

But more times than not, our playful banter helped alleviate tension between the child and me and underscored the nonnegotiable reality that I, their mother, was indeed the boss.

I knew it.

They knew it.

And all was right with the world. Well, at least for a good half hour or so.

## Let God's Promises Motivate You

I've always said I wouldn't speak or write about any stage of mothering that I had not lived through and/or failed at. Allowing this to be my plumb line when it comes to book writing, speaking topics, and advice doled out via television, radio, and personal email and phone conversations, I am assured of two things:

1. It will keep me grounded and free me from any I'm-Miss-All-That musing when accolades come my way. After all, it's hard to get away from some of the confessions I've committed to print and DVD production!
2. It gives me cause to boast in the One who promises to be faithful to me and my children—regardless of what I do.

I was reminded of this time and time again while navigating the past four years with my daughter. To say we had a tumultuous journey is an understatement if there ever was one, what with days and nights marked with raised voices, accusations, tears of frustration and anger, weariness, hopelessness, desperate prayers, and silence. The silence was the worst. During those times especially I returned to familiar Bible truths and reread God's promises pertaining to life and faith and just about everything else I could possibly throw at him. I was desperate for God, and these words comforted me time and time again:

The LORD himself watches over you!
   The LORD stands beside you as your protective
   shade.
The sun will not harm you by day,
   nor the moon at night.

The LORD keeps you from all harm
   and watches over your life.
The LORD keeps watch over you as you come and go,
   both now and forever.

Psalm 121:5–8

The LORD is a shelter for the oppressed,
   a refuge in times of trouble.
Those who know your name trust in you,
   for you, O LORD, do not abandon those who
   search for you.

Psalm 9:9–10

Show me the right path, O LORD;
   point out the road for me to follow.
Lead me by your truth and teach me,
   for you are the God who saves me.
   All day long I put my hope in you.
Remember, O LORD, your compassion and unfailing
   love,
   which you have shown from long ages past.
Do not remember the rebellious sins of my youth.
   Remember me in the light of your unfailing love,
   for you are merciful, O LORD.

Psalm 25:4–7

A house is built by wisdom
   and becomes strong through good sense.
Through knowledge its rooms are filled
   with all sorts of precious riches and valuables.

Proverbs 24:3–4

A wise woman builds her home,
but a foolish woman tears it down with her own
hands.

Proverbs 14:1

When nothing else makes sense—God's Word does. Make your own list of Bible promises to cling to when you're in need of some courage or comfort. Maybe you're not quite sure how to go about this, but it's as easy as looking up the word *promise* in the concordance portion in the back of most study Bibles. If your Bible does not have such a study reference, look for the word in the index. And should you strike out there too, I strongly recommend you purchase a new Bible and specifically look for one with such a concordance. In the meantime, you can make your way over to BibleGateway.com and do a quick word search in most any translation of the Bible. You can also purchase two incredible written resources which will help you on your way:

*God's Inspirational Promises* **by Max Lucado.** With Scripture verses arranged topically for easy access, this is one of the bestselling promise books of all time. This little book has sold more than 700,000 copies since its first printing in 1996. Filled with inspirational promises about valuing others, anger, suffering, and more, this is a promise book filled with comfort and guidance that you'll turn to again and again during times of need.

*God's Promises for Women* **by J. Countryman.** This collection of Scripture touches on God's faithfulness and sovereignty and offers an elegant reminder of the joy and hope found in the Lord. Profiles of the dynamic women of faith in the Bible encourage women to attain God's best in their own lives.

There will be numerous times as a mother when the words and advice of friends, experts, and family will ring hollow and ineffective.

There will be numerous times as a mother when the last thing you either want or need is one more person telling you what you should think or feel or do.

There will be numerous times as a mother when you come to the end of yourself.

When these times come, let me urge you with everything within me to run to the wisdom of the Bible. Run—don't walk—to the book of Proverbs, which so aptly lays out principles to guide our children's lives and ours as well. Run—don't walk—to the book of Psalms, which so honestly expresses crushing emotions of grief, anger, frustration, failings, as well as brilliant declarations of hope, peace, contentment, and the unfailing love of God toward each and every one of us.

Such truth, God promises, will help us become rooted, established, and built up in knowledge and wisdom and ultimately bring about a richer, more thankful life.

## Shoot for Consistent, Informed, and Fair

I once wrote of being consistently inconsistent as a mom. Unlike God, I could be quite capricious in my maternal dictates. Hormones rather than wisdom often ruled my thoughts and words when my children were much younger, and it wasn't uncommon for me to rule first and think later. I didn't much like myself when I acted in that manner, and neither did my children—and rightfully so, in many cases.

Sometime before Patrick was born in 1995, I decided to change. I wanted Kristen and Ricky Neal to know what it was like to have a mom who was a bit more relaxed in her "be the boss" ways, so I began to incorporate one important rule of thumb in my day-to-day maneuverings.

My yes meant yes and my no meant no more consistently.

Instead of shooting from the hip or making an off-the-cuff decision, I began to stop and listen to the children. I made myself gather necessary details regarding the matter at hand and tried my best to make rulings based on informative details—rather than emotions, hormones, or the fact that one child was annoying me more than the other.

You can do the same.

Learn to divorce yourself from the emotion of the moment or the personality of the child in the moment and more thoughtfully assess what is actually going on and being said. Force yourself to hear your children out (to the One Tough Mother degree necessary—after all, they can totally work us in our efforts at being more thoughtful), and even pray for the wisdom of that wise king named Solomon before dispensing your judgment.

Don't apologize either for your yes or for your no.

Let it be.

## Say What You Mean and Mean What You Say

In our family one is not allowed to hem or haw. You have to say what you want because no one is going to attempt to read your mind. For instance, if you were eating breakfast with us and I asked, "Would you like some honey for your biscuits?" and you replied, "I dunno," or "I guess," I would kindly repeat the question, pause, and then add, "Yes or no?"

Consider some of the common phrases you either speak to your children or respond with as they speak with you—evasive words and elusive phrases such as, "We'll see," "Maybe later," or the truly tuned-out commuter phrase of "Uh-huh."

"Mom, can I get a new video game at GameStop today?"

*"We'll see."*

"Mom, can I get on MySpace for a while?"

*"Maybe later."*

"Mom, is it okay if I lick all the interior windows of the Yukon?"

*"Uh-huh . . ."*

(Can you say non-committal responses?)

Technically, this shouldn't be all that difficult to do, but then again, we're attempting to reprogram our verbal reflexes after years and years of being on autopilot. Admit it, moms, you don't even hear (or remember) a certain percentage of responses you utter during the day! They don't stick with you, and they certainly aren't sticking with your children. Hence the need for a little One Tough Mother authority in our words. Say exactly what you mean and be the boss.

"Mom, can I get a new PlayStation game at GameStop today?"

*"Not on your life!"*

"Mom, can I get on MySpace for a while?"

*"Yes, I'll set the timer for thirty minutes, and then you're off."*

"Mom, is it okay if I lick all the interior windows of the Yukon?"

*"Are you completely nuts? No . . . absolutely no."*

No more wishy-washy responses allowed, girls. If your kids are going to take you seriously, they need to hear decisive answers from you.

Being the boss doesn't always come easily—or naturally. But if you buckle down and work on the principles we've examined here, you'll be on your way to claiming the authority that's yours as the mom.

# 4

# Diagnosis: Average

## Nonnegotiable #2:
## Delight in Your Perfectly Ordinary Child

A word from your author before we begin:

(Ahem.) I, Julie Barnhill, under severest threat of author duress and reader accusation—*i.e.*, *"lack of originality"*—do solemnly swear hereunto to abstain from any and all insipid, rhyming mention of the tired and overused word *extraordinary* (hereby referred to as *E*) in conjunction with *ordinary* in the chapter following, so help me God.

Moving right along . . .

Not too long ago, I was interviewed by Dr. James Dobson at Focus on the Family in Colorado Springs, Colorado. I was looking forward to meeting with his radio staff and producers, but to be completely honest, the ten- to fifteen-minute window of conversation he so graciously allows guests before the actual interview was what I most eagerly anticipated.

Some close girlfriends of mine had half-jokingly forwarded parenting questions they wanted me to sneak in and get answered. I deferred their requests as I was smack-dab in the middle of writing *One Tough Mother* and had a few inquiries of my own:

"Dr. Dobson, would you be so kind as to finish writing my book?"

"Dr. Dobson, may I have a job hosting a show for Focus on the Family?"

"Dr. Dobson, may I call you once a week for advice until my twelve-year-old makes it through puberty, my seventeen-year-old passes Algebra II, and my nineteen-year-old figures out God's will for her life?"

No big deal, really. Just little questions like that.

So on an unseasonably warm November afternoon, I found myself having that highly anticipated conversation. One of the show's expert broadcast producers joined us as we discussed the phenomenal listener response and feedback to a previous interview we'd done as well as each of our current book projects (I was trying to sell him on an interview for this book!).

Dr. Dobson asked about the premise of *One Tough Mother*, and I shared with him the chapter titles. After hearing this one, he laughed and said, "Julie, I wrote something about that in a book of mine eight or nine years ago." He then went on to summarize his take on the matter. What he said went something like this:

> When a husband and wife find out they are expecting, all they want to be assured of for the following nine months is that everything is average—that everything is normal like every other ordinary, normal, healthy pregnancy. As soon as the baby is born, all those parents want to know is that their baby is average: ten fingers, ten toes, two eyes, one nose. But then, from that point on, they don't want their

child to have anything to do with average. Average just isn't good enough.

That discussion pretty much killed my "will you finish my book" request, but it sent me shouting to the heavens knowing that I was indeed onto something! Honestly, I'm ready to throw up on or chuck a heavy object at the next author or Web writer who draws a line of demarcation between a mother raising a child of *E* value or one *merely* settling for something less.

Enough of that, I say.

I'm tired of reading it, hearing it, and seeing it splattered on covers of parenting books. Ugh. What's so wrong with a woman simply desiring to raise an ordinary, good old garden-variety child anyway?

That's right, girls, I said it and asked it—and quite loudly, despite the deceptively demure font style and size. What's wrong with a mother purposely raising an ordinary, usual, normal, without distinction (to everyone but the child's own mother!) child?

When did this inane aversion to anything less than stellar! and phenomenal! and distinctive! (heaven help us if our child doesn't stand out by age three weeks) overtake sensibility and put us on the Wacko Mommy Track of overachievement and online shopping mall purchases of a Baby Einstein Mozart accompaniment–playing teething ring?

## An Ordinary Author's Ordinary Kids

Disclaimer: I have three children and asked their permission to commit the following observations to print. They agreed on the condition that a healthy increase to their royalty cut was put in place. Done. After all, without them

I have zero material and would have to start writing about my sister-in-law Trisha's kids.

So here it 'tis: none of my children have ever been described as *E.*

Not one.

None of the three ever qualified for "gifted" school programs.

None of the three joined MENSA after scoring off the charts on a standardized state achievement test.

None of the three learned to speak at age six weeks or potty trained themselves before year one.

None of the three were scouted by sports agents.

None of the three were academically bored in their math or physics classes. (Oh, wait, none of the three ever attempted a physics class.)

None of the three have ever quoted (with annoying accuracy or cuteness) Scripture back to me or their father after being disciplined.

None of the three starred on their own television program.

None of the three begged us to allow them to work as teenagers so they could save vast amounts of money for their future college needs.

None of the three have filled up the gas tanks regularly.

None of the three have ridden hundreds of miles during a family trip without complaining or purposely hurting a sibling.

Nope.

Not a one.

Kristen walked at eight months but couldn't find her way out of a snug turtleneck shirt until around age five.

Ricky Neal rode a two-wheel bicycle sans training wheels a little past his second birthday but pointed to his belly button when asked "Where's your nose?" long past the time his father and I liked.

And while Patrick demonstrated empathic understanding toward his older sister and patted her shoulders and said, "It's okay," before his first birthday, a few months later he stood in a second-story window, pressed himself against its tenuous screen, and shouted to his freaked-out older brother staring slack-jawed at him twenty feet below, "Look, Ricky! I'm Spiderman!"

It seems I (and their father) have raised three ordinary, garden-variety kids. Ordinary, my friend—gloriously and nerve-jarringly ordinary.

But despite this gloriously ordinary reality, all three have somehow managed to . . .

tie their shoes,

speak in full and complete English sentences,

use the potty appropriately (gads! At what age as a mother will I finally quit saying potty?),

carry on animated and entertaining discussions with peers and adults who will give them the time of day,

pass required math classes—*eventually*,

back talk, sass, and be royal pains to deal with for varying amounts of time,

question, consider, and individually embrace Christian faith,

think they know more than their dad or me on any given day,

scratch chicken pox lesions and have the scars to prove it,

prefer to watch me work rather than do it themselves, and

only perform some work upon threat of losing driving privileges, cash, or time MSN IM-ing with friends.

The kids come by it naturally.

Rick's and my gene pools are fraught with ordinary cells, and I'm willing to bet the same could be said for yours. Yet so many of us cringe at the word when it comes to describing our children or the nature of our family unit.

We can't seem to relax and consciously allow our children to be ordinary. Think about it: how often have you attended a mothering conference or read a parenting book or watched Dr. Expert pontificating on television and been told that it is perfectly sound and wise to aspire to raise ordinary kids?

Not very often, eh?

A quick Amazon.com search and I can purchase parenting tomes instructing me how to raise:

courageous kids
faith-filled kids
good kids
money-smart kids
emotionally intelligent kids
sensory-smart kids
socially confident kids
motivated kids
"gifted" kids
*E* kids
musical kids
successful kids
well-behaved kids
resilient kids
adopted kids
healthy kids
confident kids

Notice anything or *anyone* missing?

It's as if we fear that in admitting the ordinariness of our children and that of ourselves and family, we will somehow be accused of grabbing hold of the lowest rung of expectation and hanging on for dear life.

It's as though allowing ourselves to consider the actual *gift* of being ordinary (remember Dr. Dobson's words?) is something akin to woefully neglectful mothering—thereby culminating in our raising children who run the risk of being called the equally disdainful *A* word—*average*.

Shiver upon shiver!

And perhaps the granddaddy example of all time for this is the not-so-humble Christmas newsletter.

Is there anything more insane or relentless than the annual tidal wave of emailed or USPS missives declaring the anything-but-ordinariness of children most of us don't even know? Oh, sure, we went to high school with their mother or maybe worked together six years ago with their dad, but it's not like we kept up with each other—or even wanted to. Nevertheless, year after year that newsletter finds its way to our mailbox or inbox and it reads something like this:

Merry Christmas from the Anything But Ordinary Family!

Wow! Can you believe it's already December 1st and another year is coming to a close? But what a year it's been. The boys (Chip and Dale) were accepted into Harvard University and we were told they were the first set of twins in the school's recent history to score 800 on each section of the SAT Reasoning Test as well as on the SAT Subject Tests. The boys were working with an international mission team in a third-world country when the Harvard admissions department called to give them the good news.

While the boys head off to Harvard, our sweet little Melissa continues to do well with supermodeling. You may have seen her on the November cover of Vogue or perhaps W? It's hard to believe she's come so far in a little less than three months of deciding to give it shot. Of course, her high school studies are still important to her, so at her request we hired a full-time academic consultant to guide her in her primary areas of interest: bioethics and international diplomacy.

Our youngest, ten-year-old Derrick, is currently finishing his second book manuscript (watch out Christopher Paolini!) and has decided to give his entire six-figure advance to a local food bank. And we all enjoyed watching Derrick as he played the lead in an off-Broadway production of Oliver this past fall.

Meanwhile, here on the home front things are pretty much the same.

Doug is still working in pharmaceutical research and is on the brink of discovering a cure for nearly everything that can kill you. Once that happens, he's going to take some much deserved time off and sail around the Sea of Cortez with three of his best friends: Brad Pitt, John Grisham, and Tony LaRussa.

And then there's me—not too much to report, same old, same old, really. I'm still an investment broker managing the wealth of 90 percent of Time magazine's most influential people; a classroom volunteer at the local Montessori school; small group leader for teen girls; translator at the United Nations; lactation consultant for the LaLeche League; and an instructor for Pilates, which I love doing as it helps me relax and maintain a size 2.

So here's wishing you the brightest and most blessed Christmas wishes!

Oh. My. Word.

So how many letters of a similar nature have you received over the years? Or perhaps you've written one or two like it instead? My, my, my. It is a most peculiar obsession, wouldn't you agree?

If I'm not mistaken, it was back around 1998 when I was first graced with such a letter. The children were ten, eight, and three years of age, and after finishing the maternally documented litany of successes I wanted to do one of two things: cry and/or slap the mother who sent it to me.* Year after year I continued to receive these Christmas wrap-up postings until finally I couldn't take it any longer. I had to do something—I had to contribute in some way to this skewed communication forum. So I decided to write my own Christmas newsletter, and I was going to do it Julie style: real and slightly snarky. It read something like this:

*Please note: rarely does a father write said newsletters. Whatupwitthat?

Merry Christmas from the Thank God This Year Is Over Family!

Gads! Can you believe it's only December 27th?! What a year this has been. Our oldest child (Kristen) succumbed to a serious case of Senioritis and became a total pain to live with. Compounding her sickness was a nauseating countdown to her ever liberating birth year of "eighteen." Ah yes, the magical eighteen that somehow grants the former downtrodden and repressed seventeen-year-old permission to "live my own life" and "do whatever I want to do." With Mom and Dad's money, of course.

While Kristen attempts to map out her life plans sans parents and parents' money (do we look completely stupid?), our middle child Ricky Neal continues with his sabbatical from academic studies. I told him he needed to ACT a little more interested in his future, but he just SAT down and reasoned it out with his dad and me. "Lighten up, folks. I don't need to worry about grades because I'm going to play in a band." We're thrilled, just thrilled.

Our youngest, Patrick, received more detentions during the first half of his fifth grade year than our daughter did over the entire course of her academic life. And he is, of course, extremely proud of said feat, and Rick and I are almost too tired to care. Both boys are playing sports this year, and I'd rather stick a pencil through both eyeballs than sit through another round of freezing cold football and hard wooden bleacher seats for basketball.

Meanwhile, here on the home front things are pretty much the same.

Rick still watches inordinate amounts of Andy Griffith, yells at the TV when political pundits come on, and leaves his fingernail clippings laying around on a nearby end table, thereby ensuring my leaving the room and finding something else to do—like eating.

Ah yes, then there's me—not too much to report, same old, same old, really. I'm still not a size 2.

So here's hoping next year is better.

We are an obsessed mothering culture scared to death of being perceived as anything less than utterly and totally conscientious. It's not enough to believe and know we did the best we could as a mother despite obstacles—no, a mother who fears the ordinary and average must move heaven and earth and settle for nothing less than nothing less.

Playing classical music to babies in utero.

Waving flashcards to infants.

Breastfeeding for at least one year.

Ice skating, horseback riding, swimming, and soccer lessons—all for one child.

Early exposure to musical instruments.

Preschool prep classes.

Limiting video/television viewing.

Reading books aloud—lots and lots and lots of books.

Finding opportunities for social interaction for your baby, toddler, preschooler.

But settling for nothing less day after day and year after year can make one very weary.

So here's what I'd like to propose: let's stand up as One Tough Mother and refocus our time and energy and dreams on raising and discovering the wonderfully ordinary children living in our homes. The best way to do this is to start asking some simple, ordinary questions of yourself, your spouse, and your children. There is no particular science to this, mind you. I simply desire for you to get to know yourself and those you love utterly and completely a little bit deeper. As we hear one another's answers and consider our own responses, I believe we will find it impossible not to see the wonder and glory wrapped up in each of our ordinary lives.

For those mothering newborns, well, give it a little time (unless, of course, you are the mother of an *E* child who can speak in full sentences at eight weeks) and write down your own responses to share with your spouse, girlfriend, or older child.

If you have older toddlers and children in grade school or high school, use the questions as conversation starters at the dinner table or while you go about your evening bedtime ritual. (By the way, if screaming up the stairs and telling your child, "Just shut your door and go to sleep!" *is* your evening bedtime ritual, well, that's more ordinary than you may think.)

You'll find all sorts of questions appropriate for varying ages listed. You're an intelligent woman and have somehow managed to parent thus far without my input, so I'm fully trusting in your ability to figure out the who, what, when, and where of it all. It (almost) goes without saying that you'll want to build upon each one and allow the questionee to answer as fully as possible. (I'm smiling thinking of those of you with chatty four-year-olds.) Just get them answered one way or another and as you do, listen—really listen—to the "these are my ordinary world" thoughts.

And for goodness sakes, enough with the steroid-induced Christmas newsletters already!

What is your favorite animal?

If you could be any animal, what would you be?

What has happened in your life that you never expected to happen?

What is one thing you have done that you are really proud of?

When are you happicst?

What is your favorite TV show?

What is one of your favorite movies?

What is one of your favorite books? What character do you like best and why?

What is your favorite food, and who cooks it for you?

What do you like to do on your birthday?

What is your favorite holiday?

What is the best Christmas gift you've received? What Christmas gift have you most enjoyed giving to someone?

What is the best gift you've made for someone else?

What are you afraid of?

Which do you do more—smile or cry?

Have you made any new friends in the last year?

Have you lost any old friends in the past few months?

What would you like to do more of?

What should you do less of?

What makes you sad?

What is the first thing you remember as a child?

What was your happiest/saddest time as a child or adult?

What is your favorite color?

What is your favorite food?

What is the most trouble you ever got into?

What is the best thing that ever happened to you?

What is the most memorable event in your life?

What kind of sports or musical instruments do you or
would you like to play?
Who has influenced you the most in your life?
Who was your worst teacher?
Who was your best teacher?
Who is your best friend?
What are some of your favorite clothes to wear?
What is the best thing that has happened to you?
Have you ever been in trouble at school? If so, why?
Where would you like to travel?
What is your favorite place you have traveled to?

Now I'd like to allow you space to write down a few questions of your own, perhaps one or two that your child came up with or something which wasn't covered in the list above. So here are a few lines. Fill them as you like, or, as some ordinary readers are wont to do, think about adding something but forget about it by the time you turn the page!

_____

_____

_____

_____

_____

I hope that your discussions soon lead you to realize that ordinary isn't boring or meaningless or unworthy. Far from it. The sacred resides in the ordinary, in . . .

a child's laugh,
the pull of a brush through a daughter's hair,
a well-hit ball off a T-ball stand,
the aroma of a baby's freshly washed nape,
the sputtering sound of frying bacon,

a wave of the ocean, determinedly followed by another
    and another,
a toddler's squeal of delight,
a daughter dancing on her father's shoes,
the scent of sweaty boys roughhousing in a family
    room,
languorous conversations with a teenage daughter after
    curfew has been met,
grandparents bragging on their grandchild,
grandchildren napping beside their Papa,
the repeated bedtime story refrain, "I'll love you forever,
    I'll like you for always . . . ,"
blueberry buckle stains on a freshly laundered bib,
a three-year-old hiding in a kitchen cabinet,
the slobbery wide-open kiss of a nine-month-old,
the pale sheen of a newborn's fingernails,
a student council campaign speech proudly composed
    and confidently delivered by a sixth-grade son before
    a student body,
bathtub rings proving a six-year-old's day spent playing
    outside,
damp footprints on ancient pine flooring,
hand after hand of Go Fish and Old Maid,
beater blades licked clean of batter,
a nerve-racking first piano recital conquered,
a nursing babe's arm outstretched toward his mother's
    smiling face,
"big boy" underwear,
teenage sons renting their first tuxedos,
teenage daughters applying liquid eyeliner,
husbands making love to their wives,
and One Tough Mother delighting in her gloriously
    ordinary child.

# 5

# Analyze This

## Nonnegotiable #3:
## Stop Tinkering with the Inane

If I were the owner of a magic wand which wrought miracles of the truly miraculous sort I would immediately use it to accomplish two things:

1. Rid the world of certain unsightly fleshly appearances.
2. Get moms to see the big picture in their mothering.

And here's how I'd do it.

First, with wand and determination in tow, I'd make my way to the nearest shopping mall, find the highest point inside the building, and while gazing down upon teeming masses of female teens and preteens, I'd wave my wand once—twice—three times, even, and magically increase the width of low-rise waistbands on all adolescent girls a minimum of three inches.

And you know what else I'd do? While I was there, I'd make my way through the congested aisles and personally whap said wand up against the heads and hips of adult women-slash-mothers trying to cram *waaaaay* post-teen body parts into casings of unforgiving denim. *(What are they thinking?)*

\*Folds of loose, flabby, or distressed skin flopping over pre-miracle waistbands.

Ah! No more thong-baring backsides to unwillingly behold.

No more inner tube of truth\* advertising the female indignity of following yet one more *really* bad fashion trend.

No more need to place a mall blindfold over the eyes of my seventeen- and twelve-year-old sons. Such wonders, such miracles. With that done, I could move on to accomplishment number two, for all is as it should be—stowed, covered, age-appropriate, and "The Gap" referring once again to the name of a clothing store only.

Accomplishment number two—getting moms like you and me to see the bigger picture when it comes to motherhood—is going to be a little trickier. Why? Because, you see, it has to do with the fact that in the midst of being quite possibly the most literate, workshop-educated, best-selling book-learned, and www.something information-downloaded mothering generation since time began, we have managed to lose our maternal confidence, maternal authority, and, dare I propose, ever-lovin' maternal brains to those I refer to as The Others.

Now who, you ask, are The Others?

Well, The Others could be just about anyone—your mother, sister, neighbor, opinionated friend—but are in all likelihood the voices and opinions of an expanding consortium of expert parenting voices with highly visible marketing campaigns, book releases, and television shows buttressing said expert status as well as the limitless, mind-boggling information available to mothers at the click of a mouse.

Case in point: consider the plethora of popular network and cable television programs made up of take-charge English nannies and parenting experts swooping into homes much like yours and mine and rescuing parents—*mothers* in particular—from out-of-control spawnlings. Week after week, parents (*mothers* in particular) with college degrees and seeming savvy business sense find their messy parenting lives metamorphosed by a prescription sheet of commonsense do's and don'ts. Week after week, parents (*mothers* in particular) rediscover their confidence, authority, and ever-loving brains as the result of a complete stranger stepping into their lives for a few short days, assessing the shortcomings of their parenting (*mothering* in particular) dynamics, and miraculously shoring up more emotional, physical, and maternal reserves.

Case in point number two: if you can access the Internet, dog-ear this page and make your way to Google.com. Type in the keyword *motherhood* and click. (I also clicked the blue definition button to see just how Google defines motherhood. Here it is: the state of being a mother, the qualities of a mother, and mothers considered as a group.) In less than 0.05 seconds, 19,800,000 hits will be listed for you to research and gorge yourself upon should you have the time or tenacity (nearly twenty *million*, ladies!).

The Others have a lot to say. And while there's certainly nothing bad or inherently wrong with their radio programs, *New York Times* best-selling releases, or blog sites offering commentary on boobs, breastfeeding, and binkies—hey, it can make for entertaining television and humorous, thought-provoking reading while you work the sleepless baby third shift—the glowing light emanating from the screen of our HDTV or iMac reveals the common current state of motherhood which should not and cannot be overlooked or dismissed.

Somewhere between dilated cervixes, adoption proceedings, oozing diapers, angry toddlers, infected milk ducts, overzealous potty training, Mommy and Me playgroups, Suzuki music lessons, fertility shots, and reading *Love You Forever* for the three-hundredth time, we have become a mothering generation tinkering with the inane.

We are enamored with details.

We ponder the imponderable.

We read a few million of the aforementioned Google hits, hoping, perhaps, someone else has pondered better than we.

We mull, ad nauseam, over what we're to *do* as a mother and don't seem settled in our mothering skin until we've charted, blocked, considered, documented, and examined the most microscopic minutia of having and raising children.

We are craaaaazy, to put it in the most simple of terms.

And that's why I'm digging for my wand, which has settled deep within the confines of my hobo bag. It's past time to move forward with the second accomplishment I wanted for us to meet: getting a bigger picture about mothering and stopping all the overanalyzing one is prone to do as a mom. All right, my wand's here in my right hand . . . now keep your eyes on the page as I move it back and forth, connecting with each Tinkering with the Inane Mother who may feel as though her head and motherhood are about to explode.

Can you feel anything yet?

A slight tingle or warm, pleasing sensation, perhaps?

(Oops, I think that was the baby, actually. Why don't you change your pants and his diaper and we'll pick up from there?)

Okay, how about now?

Anything?

Hmm, it appears it will take a little something more than fairy tale magic if we are to make headway in this area; maybe some good old-fashioned "I have been there" truth will help out. Take it from me; I know what it's like to live at both ends of the tinkering spectrum. In years past I sought and researched for an elusive someone to tell me what to do and say, when to do and say it, and how to feel about having done and said it. I also chose at some point in the mothering game to deliberately step up and trust my own voice of leadership and authority.

And you know what? My kids have turned out right decent.

Not perfect.

Not Stepford clones of one another.

And not without foibles and character flaws with which they'll each have to contend through adulthood and (oh, happy day!) their own parenting adventures.

But they are "right decent" because I have lived and breathed, fought and relinquished, worried and stewed, bawled and prayed for help over crippling minute worries.

Little else rattles our confidence and ability to trust in our fundamental checklist of maternal common sense quicker and with more angst-ridden power than inordinate attention to details that don't really matter. And little else falls quicker to the wayside in the midst of those details than the soothing and raucous relief of laughter and pure unabashed enthusiasm for life as it is right here, right now.

I've been there, and I know you don't have to wait for some television crew to invade your home to get a grip on what you're doing as a mom.

I've been there, and I know you don't have to purchase every parenting book that comes down the self-help shelf line (although I do appreciate your picking up this one).

I've been there, and I know you certainly don't have to settle for living with children through days, weeks, months, years, and decades (yes, decades) without knowing you're doing a fantastic job and knowing what it's like to thrive.

See, some of you reading these pages are still miffed beyond belief that your tinkered, well-thought-out, well-constructed, well-detailed birth plan didn't quite pan out the way it was supposed to. You wanted and expected to control:

a) when you conceived,
b) how the pregnancy would go, and
c) the degree of discomfort and pain you would deal with come delivery.*

*Some of us didn't discover until baby #3 that any of this was even possible.

However, some of our eggs didn't get the memo and failed to show up for conception.

Others of us found ourselves cradling the porcelain pedestal far more often than our day planners or BlackBerrys had allowed.

And more than a few had a baby fail to follow through with the "No more painful than a difficult gas cramp" labor and delivery contract clause. That child nearly split you asunder in the process! (I like that word, *asunder*. Makes the nonbirthing male world stand up and take notice. Well, clasp their knees together in confused empathy and take notice, that is.)

A mother's tinkering list can and does go on and on and on . . .

potty-training
pacifiers
teething

first haircuts
bottle vs. breast
sleep issues
school readiness
television viewing
dating guidelines
curfews
Internet use

You name it, it's not only being analyzed, I guarantee you it's been overanalyzed by some mother, somewhere. When I traveled and spoke to mothers in China, Hungary, Austria, and Germany, time and time again they expressed concerns and worries about the very things listed above. And more than a few of them, despite their age or the number of children they were raising, expressed their unsettled lack of focus and confidence about what was really important.

Perhaps you aren't quite convinced? Okay, then work with me for just a moment, if you will. Here's where I need you to stop your brain from thinking whatever you're currently thinking and gestate on some simple questions:

What is the messiest room in your house and how long would it take you, and you alone, to clean it?

What jean or blouse size do you wish you were?

When is the last time you finished a complete thought or sentence?

What did the priest, pastor, or rabbi speak about at the last worship service you attended?

What do you know you "should" do when it comes to your faith but don't do?

How many baskets of unfolded laundry are currently stacked behind your closed attic stairwell door? (Gulp.)

How often do you get to simply sit down and relax . . . distraction free?

Chances are, those seven questions will spark further thoughts. So now close your eyes and consider the following:

How much time,

    energy,

        joy,

            space,

                rest,

                    grace,

                        and tension

would you and I be released from and to if we could just take captive the myriad infinitesimal distractions of our lives?

It's a big thought—go ahead, close your eyes and ponder it awhile. I'll be here waiting when you return.

Oh, the insane weariness of a life held hostage to distractions—even worthy ones! But that's exactly what I have allowed in my own life as a mom. Getting caught up in the microscopic doings and worries of details (none of which will come as a big surprise to any of you reading): times table drills, permission slips, spelling lists, vaccination schedules, college applications, potty training tactics, and on and on it goes.

Flitting place to place, thought to thought; catching life, doing life, seeing life through static peripheral vision rather than setting my gaze firmly and determinedly on what lies square ahead.

All too often my inability (or unwillingness) to differentiate the profound from the pedestrian led to those distractions becoming weights—strongholds, if you will—that I eventually considered bigger and more powerful than anything I or God could possibly remedy.

Now that kind of mental and spiritual capitulation, my friend, will not only wear you down but leave you bent, broken, and bedraggled to boot. One Tough Mother looks said distractions square in the eye (remember, we have an eternal goal in sight as we make our way along) and decisively determines, *profound or pedestrian?* She asks, *Is this something that even warrants my attention? And if it is, what can I do about it?*

Oh, the things we spend our lives trying to fix or figure out or change or influence! You'll avoid a lot of weariness of body and soul if you take hold of this One Tough Mother attribute.

Pardon me, but I really don't think you need one more expert telling you what to do or not do. Nor do I want to come across as one more author who sets out to convince you she has all the answers. I do not. But these things I possess: experience, failure, confidence, obnoxious humor, a willingness to both teach and learn—and a desire to do nothing more than connect with you as a woman and mother.

I want you to get off the analysis couch of tinkering with the inane and move forward. Put The Others and the overanalyzing aside and focus on the big picture. Focus on your particular family's needs, and stand firm knowing your One Tough Mother convictions rather than constantly changing course based on what others say or think or imply or speak or, gasp, even write.

# 6

# Non, Nyet, Nada, Nein, Nulle

## Nonnegotiable #4: Say No Like You Mean It

Tiny grunts give way to babbling, and babbling to semi-coherent sounds, and semi-coherent sounds to a word—your child's first word. Oh, my! You've waited for this moment since they were born. Wondering—pondering—delighting in the possibilities of what word it will be.

Maybe it'll be Momma or some variation thereof. And let's be candid with one another here—their first word really *should* be Momma. After all, we're the ones putting in the majority of time and resources, aren't we? It's only fitting we should be rewarded accordingly.

But then again, hearing them speak any word would be sweet.

So we engage our little ones in discussions as they stare rather blankly during those first few weeks and months. The inflection of our voice rises and falls while our animated expressions encourage a million little brain synapses to spark in their adorably round little heads. We talk like there's no tomorrow and ask rhetorical question after rhetorical mom-teaching-moment question. We do our part and wait, for seven to eight months laying the groundwork:

"Oh, look, it's the sun. Do you see the sun? Can you say sun?"

"What's the color of Mommy's shirt? Do you see Mommy's shirt? Mommy's shirt is red! Can you say red?"

"Oh, what's that stinky smell? Goodness, can you say *nasty*?"

Those little babbles that make our toes curl with wonder are in fact an attempt by our babies to mimic the sounds of their environment. So next time your know-it-all preteens think you've lost it because you're gooing and gawing with their baby brother, just tell them they don't, in fact, know what they're talking about. Just keep on talking, and five to ten months later, the first recognizable words will emerge. And they will usually be associated with the important people and rituals that compose the child's day-to-day life.

"Mama." (Thank goodness!)

"Dada."

"Milk."

"Dog."

"Doughnuts."

It's official. Your child is a genius, and you begin to record as many of their MENSA-worthy words as possible. I journal, document, and/or record for posterity's sake just about everything having to do with life. I'm not much of a scrapbooker (more about this in an upcoming chapter), but I love words, and the pages of my three children's baby books are filled with thousands of them—documenting the what, when, where, and how-for's of nearly everything they did and said. If you'll be so kind as to bear with me, I'd like to share just a few of my baby Einsteins' comments.

> You toddled to the living room window, looked out, and toddled back to Mommy and Daddy, saying, "Ball." You did this about six times before I finally stood up, went to the window, looked out, and saw you were pointing at the moon. (Kristen)

> You promptly clasp your hands together, bow your head, scrunch your eyes tightly shut with such intensity I'm sometimes afraid you're going to pop a capillary, and say, "Pay, pay, pay, pay." You won't stop until Daddy, Kristen, and I say these exact words: "God is great, God is good." (Ricky Neal)

> You put some of Coconut's cat food in your mouth and promptly spit it out and said, "Yucky!" You then proceeded to say "Yucky" approximately 1.3 million times for the remainder of the day—again and again and again and again. (Patrick)

Remember those days? Perhaps you're right in the middle of them even as you read these words. It really is fascinating to listen as your children develop their vocabulary. One word after another—then perhaps a two-word phrase, and you couldn't be prouder.

*Then* and only then it happens.

When you are convinced of their near-perfect creation and have perhaps *strongly* stated such thoughts to any and all moms hanging out at Gymboree class or picking up a student at the elementary school . . . then and only then *it* happens.

Your perfect child places tongue against top palate, draws lips together, and enunciates a particular two-letter word with gusto and a smirking little grin thrown in for good measure. You know what it is . . . two letters . . . one syllable . . . sounds like . . .

No.

That's right, no.

Now I'm not simply talking no for no's sake. I'm alluding to the kind of no that makes you sit up and take notice. The verbalized no that lets everyone within the sound of the *formerly* gifted child's voice aware that they know exactly what they're saying. Make no mistake about it, they own the word and they mean every two-letter word of it.

And of course I recorded the exact date and circumstances when each of my children fell from grace:

> I do believe you are the most obnoxious child in the entire universe. Today you were once again attempting to fill the toilet bowl with toilet paper. I put an end to that and had you walk in front of me toward the living room where you had about three dozen real toys to play with. As we were exiting you said, "No!" And stopped—just stopped on a dime. I insisted you keep walking, and as you did you mumbled beneath your breath, "No, Mommy, don't ever do again." Who is this child!? (Kristen, early October 1991)

> We spent New Year's at Bill and Becky's house. Bill has a collection of Case tractors which children are not allowed to play with. Somehow you got ahold of one and went running through the family room trying to keep it away from me and your dad. Your daddy told you to stop and to give the tractor back. You stopped

all right. Stopped, looked back and forth at us like a trapped animal, and then set your gaze and took off running, all the while shouting in short little breaths, "No, no, no, no, no!" (Ricky Neal, January 1, 1992)

I told you to stop kicking your foot at Coconut the cat today and you turned, squared your shoulders, stuck your pointer finger in my direction, said, "No," then commanded "You, hush." I was almost expecting you to spit green pea soup or something. (Patrick, March 3, 1996)

My children were far too comfortable, far too early, with tossing around that particular two-letter word. And over the years they've held to it with firm, stubborn conviction. (Granted, sometimes this fact pleases me, such as when they are declining opportunities to engage in illegal activities. That "no" is always appreciated. But other times, when it goes head-to-head with my will—not so much. Try not at all.)

Nevertheless, they said it confidently and quickly. And the *quickly* point really irritates me because I had to wait weeks and months to hear "mama" or "hold me." Even longer to hear one say "love you." But when it came to the word *no*? No problem. Out it came in a matter of seconds.

And I saw it forming long before it was ever spoken aloud. You know what I'm talking about; think about the day you removed an object from a set of little hands and saw a "No!" flare behind those surly toddler eyes. And don't forget all the nonverbal harbingers: passionate head-shaking, arched backs, squeals, and sundry delightfully cooperative behaviors and sounds. Make no mistake about it, their lips may have been unable to form the word, but they were saying it as sure as could be.

*Question:* why is it none of us have had to teach our children to say no?

You can scan all the tomes ever written about parenting and you'll find nary a chapter, paragraph, sentence, or dangling participle instructing you how to do so. You won't need to attend a workshop titled "Bringing Out the No in Your Child." Fact is, kids instinctively say no—and also seem to know when you are least able to handle them doing so (i.e., during worship services; in front of their adoring grandparents—your husband's parents, more specifically; or while you are sitting on the toilet in a public restroom as they jiggle the door latch open!).

*Observation in light of question:* you'd think, given the confident propensity of children to say no with such ease so early on, that mothers would be able to do the same. You'd think! But I know and you know that simply isn't always the case.

Just this morning I clicked my favorite online news site, DrudgeReport.com, and read about a three-year-old girl (and her parents) getting kicked off a flight to Florida due to her preschool antics and refusal to sit down and buckle up for takeoff. She was removed because "she was climbing under the seat and hitting the parents and wouldn't get in her seat" during boarding, AirTran spokeswoman Judy Graham-Weaver said.[1] Her mother insisted, "We weren't given an opportunity to hold her, console her or anything."[2]

Meanwhile, I'm sure, the 112 travel-worn passengers on board were probably thinking she'd fit nicely (and quietly) in an overhead storage compartment.

I've encountered my share of toddler terrorists and their wimpy mothers over the past two decades as well. There was Aidan, who kicked the back of my seat nonstop during a flight to Tampa, Florida. Two hours, and I'm still not sure which was worse—the annoying thump against my backside or the annoying blather of his mother: "No, Aidan, you need to stop; the nice lady probably (*probably?*)

doesn't like you doing that." "Aidan, honey, Mommy said no. If you want to kick something, kick me." (Okay, so I made the last one up, but she may as well have put a sign on her back and let him have at it!)

There was the spawnling from Sheol who, with his mother's nonauthoritative permission, invaded my home one quiet Tuesday morning. Upon entering he promptly made his way to my newly upholstered chair, laid down on the floor on his back, placed his dirty-shoed feet on the piece of furniture, and proceeded to spin it around and around and around and around. Good grief. I just watched, slack-jawed, all the time thinking, "Surely she's going to say something or make him stop."

The bad part was that she wasn't what I would call a girlfriend—I didn't really know her all that well. If I had, well, things would have worked out a bit differently on my end. See, I would have walked over, scooped up the three-foot reprobate, and stuck him and his mother in time-out. As it was, she was merely an acquaintance, and one attending a Bible study in my home no less. So I just watched my lovely damask-shirred chair spin around and around and around.

And I might mention the time I was speaking before an audience of two to three hundred women and a crawling baby wove his way in between my feet and drooled on them as the mom looked at me from the front row and shrugged as if to say, "Eh, what can you do with an ambitious one-year-old?" Well, let's see—you can lovingly pick the baby up (which I did), you can look said one-year-old in the face and get bowled over by his pugnacious expression (which I did), and you can then hand the baby to mom, walk back toward the stage, and resume your keynote, only to observe mom practice "catch and release." Sigh. It's all over but for firmly standing your ground and preparing for the next slobbering attack.

Here's some One Tough Mother truth: we have become a nation of emphatically challenged mothers. We've either forgotten or never acquired the verbal skills necessary to express ourselves in a forceful (and yes, healthy) manner when dealing with our children.

Our yes's are yes, but our no's?

Well, our no's are *mostly* no, unless we decide maybe it *shouldn't* be, and in that case we really mean *maybe*—or *wait and see*—but then again, we should say no, but wait a minute . . . *anyone else feeling a nervous tick in their left eyelid?*

We've unwittingly sidestepped decisiveness and rarely own our commands.

Own as in declare them without apology or second-guessing.

Own as in "I said non, nyet, nada, nein, nulle—no."

Listen, I remember engaging (and I use that term lightly) in a battle of wills with my child (the age doesn't matter, but it's even more humiliating when they're three and under). It almost seemed as though I stepped outside my body, listened to what was being said (or not said on my part) and thought, *Gads, Julie, you might want to find your backbone before breakfast tomorrow*.

Why is that?

We survived childbirth, and more than a few of you endured grueling adoption processes or drawn-out custody hearings—why then, after proving we are indeed One Tough Mother, do we wimp out when it comes time to be firm and decisive with our children? Why is it that the same woman who leads an army at work can do the direct opposite at home?

What's with us?

We're reasonably well educated.

We're fairly well read.

We're relatively self-confident in who we are as women and mothers. (Hey, we all have our days.)

We even *know better* for the most part.

So how to explain feeling (dare I admit, even looking) like a complete moron while standing in the middle of Target and trying to coerce a kid smaller than the circumference of our right thigh to listen and obey when we say no?

Oh, the humanity—oh, the emphatically challenged mothering humanity!

Well, it isn't like we haven't had a little help from our culture on this. And just so you know, I'm not about to blame an ever elusive "them" for everything or even most things contributing to our emphatically challenged status. But facts are facts, and many of the powerful voices that have guided our conversations (and actions) these past twenty-five-odd years have told us to use any word but the "no" word when directing our children. Recently I did a little online research, spoke with dozens of mothers, and looked through a couple of dog-eared books I religiously studied when first learning how to do this mothering thing over eighteen years ago.

The first book I pulled down from my bookshelf was a perennial bestseller and the first "how to" book I ever purchased. I scanned through a few pages and came to the following, which I'd highlighted and put an exclamation mark next to:

> Limit your "no's" to situations that threaten the well-being of your toddler, of another person, or of your home. . . . With each "no," always offer a "yes" in the form of an alternative.

Trust me, when Heidi, Sandee, and Arleen said limit your no's and always (*always?*) offer an alternative yes, well, you did it. After all, who was I to question them (even though I ran out of yes alternatives about fifteen seconds into any situation with my toddlers)?

I'm shaking my head as I flip through the book because I can so clearly remember feeling like I knew absolutely nothing those first five years, and I rarely took the time to consider what I thought was best or appropriate—I simply read and did what I was told. Given my propensity to follow aimlessly, I'm thankful I did not have access to the overwhelming information available online to twenty-first-century moms.

Performing a Google search using the keywords "how to avoid saying no as mom," I clicked my way over to the first site listed—AskDrSears.com—and read the following quote about one-third of the way down the page:

> Having lots of face-to-face contact in the early months makes face-to-face communication easier in the months and years to come. Some children are so impressed by body language that you can get your point across without even saying a word. An expressive mother of a connected two-year-old told us: "Usually all I have to do is glance at her with a slight frown on my face, and she stops misbehaving."[3]

I have to tell you, I laughed out loud after reading this paragraph. I can almost guarantee that mother never met a two-year-old like mine. Expressive looks, nothing. Ricky Neal would have chewed me up and spit me out in less time than it takes me to eat three hot Krispy Kremes. Dr. Sears offers excellent advice and great tips, mind you; I just found this particular mothering example to be a bit annoying and not all that realistic, given the tales shared with me by other moms with don't-give-a-rip-what-your-expression-is children.

I'm not trying to paint with some broad stroke here and say there's nothing good in any of the books, writings, or advice from the examples just given. I don't think the *What to Expect* books are evil or Dr. Sears is a charlatan or online advice is something to always be avoided. I just want us to think about why we are hard pressed to look our children in the eye and say, "No . . . because I said no."

Cultural opinions factor in, as does the parenting climate of our homes growing up. I've said it before in prior books, and it bears repeating: you can't escape or ignore the way you were raised.

You can't get around it.

You can't go over it.

You can't go under it.

You have one choice and one choice only: to go through it and deal with the details accordingly.

Perhaps as a child growing up you felt you had no voice. Someone always talked louder or made sure to keep your voice silent, and as a result you determined early on to listen, truly listen, to your children from the moment they were born. There's nothing inherently wrong with this thinking. It's understandable. But it's quite possible you've allowed a bit too much leeway and now it's your own children who seem to silence or diminish what you have to say.

What about those who can look back with penetrating hindsight and see how we played our mothers like a Stradivarius? You know who you are and what I'm referring to. Maybe you were a bit like me; my mom would say no, but I knew which buttons to push and exactly what words to speak to eventually get my way 99 percent of the time. I was determined, and as unlikely as it seems, I usually got my way without resorting to obnoxious or outwardly bratty behavior, but it was manipulation nevertheless.

Given those details, I was determined not to allow any future children of mine to get by with the same behavior. I was going to be on top of things. I was going to be Queen of the Castle.

And then I actually had children and realized that in my zeal I tended to be a bit too heavy-handed.

Sigh.

Like most things when it comes to real life, it's all about finding the happy medium. Fact is, many moms say no too little and with a tone of voice that belies any parental firmness they are hoping to convey. Other moms say no too often and with such verbal gusto that it puts off their children. The One Tough Mother goal is learning how to say no like you mean it, with a measured balance of confident grace. Here are some suggestions to help you along the way.

## You Lookin' at Me? You Talkin' to Me?

It's a no-brainer.

It's a given.

It goes without saying (almost).

One Tough Mother has to have "The Look" and "The Tone" down to an exact science.

Granted, not all children will quake in its presence (such as my middle child, Ricky). But a large percentage will—and until you know which statistical cut you have living with you, well, keep on perfecting that laser gaze that screams, "I'm serious and you do not want to mess with me." You'll also want to work on the phrasing, cadence, and inflection of any spoken words—hence "The Tone." The Look and The Tone must be used sparingly. Otherwise, not unlike the greasy overkill of butter-flavored liquid squirted a bit too freely on a pint bag of movie theater popcorn, both are rendered useless and ineffective.

Go put yourself in front of a mirror and start glaring.

Think about your own mother—or perhaps the Murle in your childhood who could send shivers through your spinal cord and obedience into your actions with a steely gaze. Go easy on the squinting, mind you. It tends to make kids laugh rather than take notice, and it can do a real number on those facial lines. Calm, cool, and totally collected is what you want. And then you can throw in a little "What we got here is a failure to communicate" verbiage to finish things off.

## Build a Repertoire of Retorts

You can let your no's be no but still mix it up a bit for variety and to keep those spawnlings on their toes. Implementing some of these responses will help you maintain the maternal firmness you must communicate but also lessen the caustic bite of saying no.

For years I have responded to any and all outrageous requests from my three children (and they know the request is outrageous but always figure it's worth a shot) with the following words: "Hmmmm, let me think about that for a minute . . ."

I then stare blankly over their right shoulder and never speak another word. Almost always I throw in just a tad of a smirk to let them know I know they know it's not going to happen.

Sound overly simplistic? Perhaps, but it has worked a thousand and one times over nearly two decades of mothering, and I've even heard a couple of my kids repeat the same process when considering something a friend or sibling has requested.

You can also say things such as:

"Not a chance,"
"Absolutely not," and
"Hello, McFly!"*

*Take a trip to the video rental store and check out *Back to the Future* to get a feel for the proper delivery of this line.

All of these phrases ultimately say no . . . without necessarily using the word no. I recognize there are mothers among us who still seek to "validate" their children's feelings and desires. I, on the other hand, don't really give a hoot about either one, but for the sake of equal opportunity repertoire training, I shall offer a delicious set of choices. So for those just starting to get their feet wet in the maternal naysayer waters, well, this can be an excellent place to start.

It's important to me that you understand that saying no doesn't automatically translate into your becoming some mean, overbearing, brutish mother from the dark side! There is a sweet spot of centered, confident, and relaxed authority we dispense as One Tough Mother. It's a matter of finding your "no language" and working with it. I'm going to give you some more options to try on for size. Say them aloud. Mix up the words as you like. But get comfortable saying no. (And don't forget, One Tough Mother incorporates The Look and The Tone effectively with each of these phrases.)

Okay, let's try one on for size—adult size to help you get comfortable. We'll work with this example: "Thank you for sharing that idea with me, and no."

Now, imagine our shopping carts passing in the baking aisle of your local grocery. Our eyes meet and I abruptly stop and say the following: "Oh, I am so glad we ran into one another! I've been thinking of you for weeks and wanted to ask you to spearhead the Committee on Committees overseeing the Subcommittee on toilet safety in our public schools. Can I count on you to do it?"

After your eyes roll back from behind your head, you have two options: say no, or go stick your head in the toilet and acquiesce. I'm thinking the first choice would work best in this situation (unless, of course, you have a passion about toilet safety in public schools). So let's deliver our

One Tough Mother line, "Thank you for sharing that idea with me, and no."

Go ahead, say it—out loud and with conviction.

Massage the words—being careful to end your sentence with a firm and emphatic tone (don't let any upward lilt tint your final word—keep it firm and emphatic).

Own the words—do not allow your body language or facial features to counteract your words.

*Thank you for sharing that idea with me, and no.*

Sweeter One Tough Mother words were never spoken.

So now you're warmed up. You've considered speaking your "no" to an adult. With the following phrases I want you to do the same thing. Except speak them aloud as you would with a young child, a junior higher, or a relentless teen.

Don't quantify.

Don't apologize.

Don't reconsider.

Just say no with more clever ways like these:

> I hear what you are saying, and no.
>
> I understand you would really like that, and no.
>
> I appreciate what I'm hearing, and no.
>
> I hear you; you could be right, and no.
>
> Thank you for asking me, and the answer this time is no.
>
> I can see that it works for you, and no.
>
> I want to please you, and no.
>
> I hear you. I care about you, and no.
>
> I really see that you want that, and no.
>
> Let me tell you a little story about a man named . . . No.
>
> By the way, do you know Noah's nickname? . . . No.
>
> Thank you, and no.[4]

## "No" in Any Language

Still looking for more ways to say "no" to your kids?
Try giving it a little international flavor:

| | |
|---:|:---|
| Italian: | no |
| Spanish: | no |
| French: | non |
| German: | nein |
| Afrikaans: | nee |
| Albanian: | jo |
| Bosnian: | ne |
| Dutch: | nee |
| Indonesian: | tidak |
| Norwegian: | nei, ikke |
| Polish: | nie |
| Portuguese: | não |
| Romanian: | nu |
| Swedish: | nej |
| Zulu: | cha |

# No Longer a Dirty Word

I remember years ago seeing a T-shirt that asked, "Excuse me, what part of NO did you not understand?" and then repeating the same phrase over and over again with my two oldest children. When they'd whine for a bowl of ice cream at 8:42 p.m. (one hour past their bedtime, mind you) I'd quickly say no. Then they'd whine some more—throw in a long, drawn-out, "But why?"—and then watch me walk out of the room, turn at the door frame, and ask, "Excuse me, what part of no didn't you understand?" They never did have a good answer.

The word no can be and is a complete sentence unto itself. No doesn't require adjectives, verbs, modifiers, or subjects. No just is and is completely comfortable standing alone—it's just you and me who have to adjust.

Author and syndicated columnist Betsy Hart poses the following in her book *It Takes a Parent*.

> As parents, I think we also have to ask ourselves, Do we believe that no is a good and protective thing?
> How do we handle the nos in our own life?
> How do our kids see us handle them?[5]

What do you think, Mom?

Do you believe asserting the no word protects your children and is good for them in light of the big picture of One Tough Mothering? Sometimes it's difficult to believe this. Especially when more often than not your no's revolve around goofy, childish requests and behaviors rather than obviously life-threatening or character-crushing choices. Who among us hasn't said no for the umpteenth time and questioned if the hassle and/or sheer monotony of doing so really added up to much?

As such, now is an excellent time to call out and identify some of the all-important good and protective benefits of our standing firm, being the mom, and saying no—even when we're not all that sure of its importance. Ms. Hart points out two specific benefits worth our consideration. First:

> For starters, there may be plenty of times when a child needs to be told no, simply because someone else's needs are rightly being put before his, or his needs, which he cannot understand, are being met when his wants are not.[6]

Saying no is a good thing because it teaches our children that the world does not revolve around them. Saying no broadens their horizons and slowly but steadily helps them develop (with your help and guidance) a more generous and giving character.

The second benefit of saying no is that it allows our children opportunity to experience irritation, frustration, anger, disappointment, sadness, and all other manner of negative emotions. This is good, good, good!

As Hart explains in her second point:

> Allowing children, even young children, to experience adversity or discontent or to have their wills crossed not only creates more peace and less exhaustion for a parent and child, but also allows children to grow in the richness of what it means to be a human being, and prepares them just a bit for the road ahead of them. Refusing to let a little one have his way in all things, even in such simple things as forgoing a puddle, getting a diaper changed, or being placed in a stroller, not only gets the family moving more easily, but trains the child and the parent to live in a world of rules (the vast majority of which are made up by someone other than himself). And many of which come down to: *no*.[7]

I'd say all those are good things, as well as naturally protective to the emotional and relational development most every mom wants to see built up in the character of her child.

So now back to Ms. Hart's earlier question: How do you handle the no's in your own life? It shouldn't surprise us in the least that our children are going to mirror, in all likelihood, the same responses to the word "no" as they see demonstrated before their eyes every day in our words, actions, and expressions.

Some of you may remember an old children's song lyric, "Oh, be careful little eyes what you see . . . Be careful little ears what you hear . . . Be careful little feet where you go." The same lyrical warning should ring within our hearts and remind us we are under the near constant scrutiny of our children's gaze. They are watching us and determining if our actions line up with our words.

How *do* you handle the no's that come your way?

Are you a complainer?

Blamer?

Pouter?

Screamer?

Have your children watched you (or possibly heard you) give a hundred and one reasons why you shouldn't have been told no?

On the other (brighter) hand, perhaps your children have witnessed you accept no with a hearty measure of contentment! Perhaps you have been the epitome of One Tough Mother under grace.

If not, it's time to practice what you preach.

Okay, moms. Let's get to it. Strengthen your backbone and hum this little ditty as a reminder as you resolve to say—and respond to—"no" like you mean it: "Oh, be careful One Tough Mother what you say . . . Be careful One Tough Mother what you do . . . Be careful One Tough Mother how you react." Your child's character depends on it.

# 7

# Scrapbooking: A Woman's Descent into Madness

## Nonnegotiable #5:
## Get a Hobby Other Than Your Kid

*Enter Rod Serling—stage, uh, page right—"All-or-nothing mother Julie Barnhill finds she has the time to put together a simple photo album of her daughter. Or so she thinks."*
*Cue* Twilight Zone *soundtrack.*

It began innocently enough—a friend invited me over to create four (yes, she said exactly four) fun scrapbooking pages using my oldest child's baby photos. I told her I'd have to find four photos before committing. She said she'd hold the line while I looked—eighteen minutes later I peeled photos from the sticky, yellow-backed album I had haphazardly stuck them in seven years prior.

Upon telling her of my find, she sighed, dropped her voice just a bit, and said quite dramatically, "Oh, Julie, that's why you really need to be here tonight. You are choosing to store your never-to-be repeated photographic memories in cheap, unsafe photo storage albums which will eventually destroy all those precious memories. You need to capture and store all of those photos and the stories they represent in a creative, meaningful, photo-safe album!" She sounded like she might start crying—she was that passionate.

Well, I had no idea I was abusing my photos and started feeling a little guilty, oddly enough. So I told her I'd be there. After all, I was always game for adding an additional hobby to my life. I quickly fixed some tomato soup and grilled cheese sandwiches for the kids. Rick wanted to know when he might be able to expect me home, as winter temperatures were frighteningly low and the weather service was calling for snow showers, possibly making roadways slick. (Translation: Rick didn't want to change more than two poopy diapers.)

Grabbing my coat, gloves, purse, four photos, and car keys, I shouted over my left shoulder as I closed our back porch door, "I'll be back pretty quick; how long can it possibly take to put together a four-page photo album?"

*Thirteen years later . . .*

No doubt about it, girls, I was sucked into a whopper of a *Twilight Zone* vortex those many years ago. I found myself in a parallel mothering universe composed of

cropping tools,
shape makers,
trimmers,
corner cutters,
oval and swirl templates,
adhesives,

tape runner,

mounting sleeves,

calligraphy pens,

decorative paper,

stickers,

and, oh yeah, photos of children.

I went to create a simple photo album for my daughter Kristen. I didn't finish even one page of the actual album. I couldn't. I was too mesmerized by the gadgets and tools and utterly enamored by other women's testimonies stating the thrill and joy of preserving family history for generations to come. I ended up driving back home with a $397.26 product bundle of scrapbooking stuff. (All-or-nothing rears its ugly head yet again!)

Preserving memories is what it's all about, my passionate friend had drilled into me. So preserve I would. With product bundle in tow, I set out to document the significant moments (according to scrapbook doctrine, *every* moment is a significant moment) of each of my three children's lives (it was going to be a bit harder to do with the youngest, as we had fewer than ten photos to use) as well as create a family album which would include photographs of Rick and me. Once those were completed, I figured, I would start on another family album highlighting holidays and birthdays.

The possibilities were endless—not so my interest.

I should have known something was amiss the very first night before writing that nearly four-hundred-dollar check. After choosing decorative background paper, stickers, and mounting tape for my four pages, I proceeded to *write* the detailed stories behind each photo.

"Julie," the traveling consultant leading the class advised, "try not to spend so much time writing about the photo—let the picture be the story." (How very Zen, huh?)

I tried, really I did, but how could I not tell the tale of Kristen's unexpected conception on our honeymoon? How could I not describe, in detail, the look upon her father's twenty-three-year-old face when he first saw the positive test result in our tiny apartment bathroom? How could I not tell the story of her hiccupping all through the pregnancy or not quote the grating comments of one particular birthing nurse whom I nearly kicked—literally—out of the birthing room?

How could I trust a picture to tell all those glorious stories?

I couldn't—so I wrote and wrote and wrote. And that's one of two reasons there are still only three completed pages in the family album I set out to create in 1994. The second reason? I couldn't seem to muster the intensity required for the long haul approach to preserving one's family history.

Truth is, I never took scrapbooking quite as seriously as some of the other moms—and I think it's altogether possible I got on their nerves. I couldn't "crop till I dropped" or "scrap myself silly." I requested lengthier breaks for eating tasty appetizers and finger foods. And I wanted to talk about something *other* than my children or theirs.

Please don't get me wrong; the women were altogether lovely, but I looked at scrapbooking as a potential hobby and a great reason to socialize both with women I knew and with those I had just met for the first time. Other women seemed to see it as a vehicle solely for investing in their children's heritage.

I'm going to spill a big secret here; I don't believe I've confessed this in any of my prior books or said it aloud at any speaking event over the past nine years. Here goes . . . *If all my interests and attention over nearly the past two decades were centered solely on the lives of my three children, I would be bored to death.*

Do you think me a complete pinhead of a mother now?

The thought crossed my mind a time or two that you would. In fact, I probably typed and deleted that confession a minimum of six times before moving on to the next sentence. The last thing I want is for you to think me shallow and selfish, but since part of the stated purpose of this book is to help us "find our backbone," I figured this was as good a place as any to stand up and say it.

Perhaps I should share with you something I always tell speaking audiences—especially those at workshops or listening to radio or television broadcasts specifically targeting mothers. You can disagree with me. You can sit there and read these words and say aloud to yourself (or to the person sitting nearest you), "I think Julie's completely full of it." It's allowed—encouraged, even. For I'm fully aware not all my observations and comments are going to ring true for every reader. I know my take on any given situation is, of course, highly influenced by certain personality quirks and life experiences.

So if you're the type of mom I would have annoyed at the weekly "Crop Till You Drop" gathering, you may want to move ahead to chapter 8 and just call this one even. If, on the other hand, you uttered a Napoleon Dynamite–worthy *"Yessssss"* upon reading my pinhead confession, continue on.

I think you can tell from the previous hundred pages that I love my children.

I love other people's children too (sometimes more because I don't have to deal with their tantrums and attitudes!). And I love and care about moms beyond measure and want to do everything I can to encourage them to be the moms they were meant to be.

I believe in being your child's cheerleader and delighting in their creations.

I don't regret one second of time I've spent wiping up spit-up, picking up dirty clothes, cooking pancakes for supper, driving kids to a bus stop so they don't have to walk in the rain, or juggling a million and one other details.

I don't resent my children in the least, but . . . I've just always believed one should retain a *sizeable* portion of her own life and interests while being a mom.

My point here is that if you turn all of your hobbies into things that center on your kids, you don't really have any hobbies that will refresh just you. And One Tough Mother needs a hobby to refresh herself. Because One Tough Mother cares about her kids—deeply, in fact—but she's not defined by her kids. When a mom's interests and hobbies are all tied to her children, she starts to be defined by her kids rather than being her own person.

We have to fight to stay interesting during these years of raising children, especially during the first seven years when they naturally require so much of our physical and mental energy and presence. It's so easy to forgo the hobbies we once pursued outside the occupation of motherhood. (Can you even remember what your hobbies were before kids?)

What did you actively pursue or engage in for play and/ or relaxation before being a mom? I posed this question to several moms at a recent event and had to laugh out loud with the mother of two children under age three as she honestly replied, "The hobby I pursued with utter abandon before kids was the very hobby that got me pregnant twice in fifteen months! Now I and my husband are both wondering if and when I'll ever want to put great sex on my list of things to pursue." (I just love real woman answers.)

Not everyone was thinking about sex—some weren't thinking about anything at all. When I asked how many of them were currently making attempts to maintain those interests to some degree, less than one quarter replied they were; a little over three fourths simply groaned and rolled their eyes.

Feel like you're in the same boat?

Let me take this time to shout out a nonnegotiable One Tough Mother truth: pursuing fun and relaxing hobbies that delight your spirit, mind, heart, and soul in the midst of motherhood is not an option, it's an imperative!

Here's where I think things get a little twisted. The definition of hobby is a pursuit that brings joy and relaxation. *Relaxation* and *joy* being the operative words here, girls. But child-obsessed mothers don't have a lot of time to relax, and how easy it is to become bored (or worse still, to become boring) when the majority of the activities requiring your time and attention are geared toward children alone.

I've met my share of interesting toddlers, junior high students, and even teenagers, mind you, but *we're* grown women, for goodness' sake. It's time we once again prioritized activities that develop our own mental, physical, and spiritual health. The simple fact is this: the more interesting we are as women (the person outside of being called Mom), the more interesting we will be to those around us. So let's start by asking ourselves two basic questions to help rebuild and revive our memory as we set a new hobby course.

*First, as a little girl, what did you enjoy doing with your free time? Has it changed much over the years?*

This one's easy for me—reading, pure reading. I can't recall a time in my life when I wasn't gleaning the pages of a storybook or perusing labels on the back of bathroom sprays, tubes of toothpaste, and perfumes. (Heads up note of advice: always have something available—magazines, humor books, even pamphlets of some sort—for the reada holics using your restroom.)

My reading habit/hobby hasn't abated a bit over the years. Friends and family still ask, "How many books are you going to buy and read this week/month/year?" And I still have no intention whatsoever of stopping. This hobby has remained of paramount importance. Other hobbies such as listening to and learning the lyrics to fresh, new song releases? Well, that pretty much came to a screeching halt in 1991. I love music—it can pull me out of the doldrums and spark creative thoughts or romance. I just haven't taken the time to maintain my interest since having children. My bad—and I intend to do something about it pronto.

*Second, when you need to relax, what do you instinctively do or pursue?*

When stress and deadlines and maternal worries threaten to make my head explode, I usually do one of four things.

One, I love to drive to Barnes & Noble and simply walk around and read book covers and explore different subject matter for hours and hours on end. This works brilliantly, for no one else in my immediate family or extended family finds this relaxing in the least bit. In fact, if I'm having a bad day and I want to lose the spouse and kids, all I have to ask is, "Who wants to go with Mom to the bookstore?"

*Poof!*

Everyone suddenly finds something else to do.

Two, I love locking the upstairs bathroom door and indulging in a prolonged hot shower where I take an inordinate amount of time shaving my legs, body scrubbing my rough parts, deep moisturizing my hair, and slathering on a facial mask that requires twenty minutes to set. After I'm done and dried off, I coat myself with more moisturizing lotion (fortysomething women can never be too soft) and then grab my cosmetics bag full of nail polishes, files, and pumice stones. I spend the next couple of hours taking care of my feet and fingers—applying applications of that Malaga Wine I spoke about in chapter 2—and then throw on a pair of ultra-soft velour sleeping pants and a sleep T-shirt. Ahhh . . . relaxed doesn't even begin to describe my state of being.

The third option I sometimes choose (and this is going to shock you) is grabbing a book I've set aside especially for days such as this and curling up in the corner of my conversational-shaped sofa to read.

And last but certainly not least, I sometimes go looking for my husband—and give the boys permission, money, and my blessing to go into town to find something to do for a while!

So how about you? How did *you* answer those questions? Was it nice to recall past days filled with hobbies and interests other than binkies, play groups, driving to traveling basketball games, and pre-prom fundraising phone calls? (If you answered no, well, you need more help than I or this book can provide.)

Here's the thing: One Tough Mothers have a hobby other than their children; they love and enjoy their children but aren't completely wrapped up in them.

One Tough Mother can and will go shoe shopping with girlfriends.

One Tough Mother still has girlfriends, for that matter!

One Tough Mother proactively learns how to incorporate her own interests and her own hobbies into her daily lifestyle and responsibilities as a mom.

So where exactly does one find a hobby if you're lacking in that department? I'm glad you asked.

I sent out a rather large email blast asking moms to send me a list of possible hobbies for you to research, consider, delve into, and enjoy. I can't help but think you'll find one or two that strike your fancy. Maybe you'll find something you once loved but have long since forgotten—sorta like me and music. Or maybe it'll be an idea entirely new and exciting! It doesn't really matter what it is as long as *you* find it interesting. Once you find something, I want to challenge you to commit your time and energy to developing it and pursuing it with the same mothering abandon you gave to breastfeeding and Mommy and Me classes. Although I can't hope to cover the gamut of hobby opportunities available to you, I've tried to give you a nice place to start. As One Tough Mother you'll never regret it.

## Suggested Hobby List

Photography (you don't even have to get all psycho about scrapbooking your pictures!)

Scrapbooking (for those of you who like to go all psycho!)

Creating an online blogging site

Interior decorating

Oil painting

Bodybuilding

Bunco

Volunteer work at your favorite organization

Film editing and creation

Pottery making

Slow-pitch softball

Singing karaoke

Cake decorating

Wine collecting

Sewing

Restoring antiques

Candle making

Computer gaming

Baking

Camping

Skiing (snow or water)

Paintball (fun!)

Walking

Deer hunting

Ballroom dancing

Long-distance running

Surfing

White-water rafting

eBay selling or shopping

Vintage dress collecting

Scuba diving

Flying lessons

Doll making

Gardening

Model trains and miniature houses

Magic tricks

Researching your family tree

Astronomy

Travel

Reading

Mountain biking

Gourmet cooking

RV-ing

Sudoku

Pilates

Composing original songs on the guitar

Breaking down and rebuilding any and all electrical gadgets

Belly dancing (I took this mom's name and number and followed up for myself!)

# 8

# Truly, Madly, Deeply

## Nonnegotiable #6: Love Them Like Crazy

Rick, my reserved and low-key to the nth degree husband of twenty years, just told me this morning that he finds the ever-increasing white strands appearing amidst my brunette head of hair to be quite sexy. I gave him a big kiss and told him I appreciated his sense of what's sexy but still intended to keep my colorist appointment. I do love that man! Strongly opinionated when it comes to politics, Rick enjoys nothing more than engaging the kids and me in spirited discussions over a home-cooked, comfort food meal of roast beef, mashed potatoes, sweet corn, rolls, and dark gravy. (We're quite health conscious, we Barnhills.)
Rick . . .

thinks I'm funny,
has never understood my obsession with books and sees no sane reason for reading five or six at one time,
considers steak to be one of the basic food groups,

enjoys a great cigar while playing nine holes of golf with his boss,

makes sure the furnace filter is replaced every thirty days,

never fails to tell me when pepper flakes are stuck between my closely spaced teeth, and

loves nothing more than discovering something that'll make me burst out laughing (television commercial, joke, YouTube video).

Yep, he's a keeper.

Kristen—first born, only daughter, and owner of a head full of gorgeous curls for which no one has yet been able to provide a genetic explanation—is beginning to come into her own in this her nineteenth year of life. I marvel as she articulates her faith more confidently, expresses her opinions more passionately (and with a bit more grace), and begins to settle into being herself. I study her features when she's home from college, seeing her father reflected in the adorable turn of her nose and similar photogenic dream angle of her jawline.

All of us sit around the living room, Kristen sprawled across my lap while I scratch her back. She speaks up and out—questioning the status quo of nearly everything (making her father and me a bit nervous), and I am reminded of the vital necessity of hammering out and truly owning what you believe.

Glancing up, she catches my eye and flashes one of her killer smiles, and my heart melts.

Ricky Neal—my six-foot-five peacemaker and up-and-coming guitar hero—has, it seems, grown up and taken on responsibility overnight. Awakening yesterday morning, I began to prepare breakfast. Hearing a disturbance upstairs, I returned to investigate; an odd roaring sound emanated from behind Ricky Neal's closed bedroom door.

I knocked.

No reply.

I gradually opened the door to shout in and ask, "Hey, what's going on in there?"

Instead, Ricky Neal swung the door open wide and resumed vacuuming his carpet. *Resumed*—as in he was vacuuming his carpet in the first place. (It's official: the Earth has stopped spinning on its axis!)

I watch this goatee-growing man-child and often find myself laughing aloud (to the consternation of those around me) as my mind processes countless memories of a headstrong, all-or-nothing toddler literally climbing the walls of our home. Now, fourteen years later, I sit and watch the *Lord of the Rings* movies (over and over again) with this charming, intelligent, thought-provoking son of mine—all the while discussing gloriously rich themes of redemption, selflessness, sacrifice, and loss.

*Whodathunkit?*

And of course there's Patrick, my third and last child, whom I rarely took to a professional photographer for documented proof of his babyhood (not that he's bitter about this or anything). Deeply affectionate, with near ebony-colored eyes, a quick-to-tan tropical skin tone, and a mouth that seldom closes conversationally, he is truly flesh of my flesh and melanin of my melanin.

I watch my son on the cusp of adolescence and he never ceases to intrigue me. He can't (won't) be bothered to throw away a dried-up, crackling cheese packet that's been sitting on his bedroom dresser the past six weeks but will, without fail, feed and water his pet snake. As he peers into said reptile's plastic abode and sneers, "Hello, Jerry,"* I laugh aloud and realize more than ever just how much I like this kid.

*Patrick had quickly picked up on the the sarcastic "Hello, Jerry'"greeting of the *Seinfeld* character Newman, which his dad and I repeatedly said over the years.

Now, lest you feel yourself threatening to retch at all of this due to saccharin overload, know this: we can be a most unlikable lot as well. Just like any family, each of us has a fair amount of "stuff," and it isn't easy to live with one another at times. For the sake of interpersonal relationships within my home, I'll refrain from publishing specific details regarding the husband and kids, but suffice it to say that when asked the best gift they could give me for Mother's Day not so long ago, I responded, "Go away."

As for me, well, I confess, living with me isn't always a picnic either. I can be pretty intense and prone to the dramatic (never would have guessed, would you?), and I have a tendency to believe I'm usually (okay, almost always) right, thereby relentlessly refusing to believe otherwise without substantial proof.*

Yeah, they (and me) can all be crabby and cantankerous at times. Nevertheless I am truly, madly, deeply in love with the four people doing this thing called life with me. And the reason I feel that way is simple: we are Barnhill and we are family.

Truly, madly, deeply. That's how I love my family. That's how crazy I am about my husband. And that's how I mother my children. My love and care for each of them is a "truly, madly, deeply" kind of thing. A truly,

*In regards to this entirely unlikable trait, Google.com has saved my family relationships on countless occasions. Here's how it works: say I'm traveling with my family and someone (say, someone who grew up listening to true classic rock, such as my husband) disagrees with my *American Idol* rendition of the lyrics to "You Just Ask the Lonely" by Journey. All I have to do is whip out my handy-dandy cellular Verizon Treo with internet access, make my way to www.google.com, tap in "just ask lonely song lyric," tap the green arrow, and . . . *voila!* prove that once again I am rig . . . *well, I'll be!* All these years I've been singing, "When you're feeling *laissez faire*, you just ask the lonely." Correct lyric: "When you're feeling *love's unfair* . . ."

madly, deeply commitment to them and to who we are as a family. A truly, madly, deeply belief that we Barnhills are the best thing God ever decided fit together. Pretty awesome stuff.

No doubt it has something to do with my adoptive past, but the sheer concept of family—having *my* family—often brings tears to my eyes. Simply hearing and recognizing Kristen's voice calling "Mom!" over the din of a crowded concert hall makes my heart jump with delight. Having my boys plop themselves beside me on Monday nights so we can watch Jack Bauer save America from extinction yet one more season—oh, man, I am *so* gone when they do that. And hungering for the sound of my husband's voice and still anticipating the touch of his hands after twenty years of marriage, well, quite frankly, it amazes me still.

I really believe one of the best things you can ever do as a mom is to stir up within your family ranks a truly, madly, deeply love and devotion for one another. When I look back at our early family years, if I have any regrets, they fall a bit more in this area than any other. It's not that I didn't do it at all—but I can see how I allowed the busyness of the children and plain old doing life weariness to sort of knock the wind out of my intentions.

Granted, I can tend to be a bit idealistic when it comes to emotional matters of motherhood, setting myself and family members up against an impossible-to-meet standard. But I still believe it's better to have a goal—an ideal to shoot toward. I've met families without such ideals and purpose, and it wasn't something I ever sought for the Rick and Julie Barnhill family.

Truth is, this subject matter really touches a soft spot in my life. I wouldn't consider myself an overly sappy woman or mother, but there's something about reveling in the family you've created via childbirth, adoption, foster care, or inadvertent happenstance that brings on the emotions. I'm smiling as I recall one such moment.

I was watching the movie *My Big Fat Greek Wedding*. Oh, my. I should have just stayed home that night.

My first mistake was going to see it by myself. Not that I have a problem with people attending movies alone—no, I have done it countless times over the years, but there are certain films I personally should not view without an emotional minder, someone like my husband or a girlfriend. But for some reason I found myself alone for a weekend, and I decided I wanted to catch it before it left the theater.

So I went expecting to laugh myself silly.

Instead I cried.

Buckets.

As well as sad little streams of never-ending tears that pool on your lower lip and drip onto the lapels of your blouse.

In a nutshell, the fictional storyline revolves around a young Greek woman (Toula Portokalos) falling in love with a non-Greek (Ian Miller) and her struggle to get her family to accept him while she comes to terms with her heritage and cultural identity.

For ninety-five minutes I took in the fictional but oh-so-real truly, madly, deeply strength and craziness of Toula's family. They were . . .

loud,
abrasive,
opinionated,
nosy,
quirky,
full of foibles,
and loving.

Surely this was my lost biological family!

(Honestly, I'm just a pathetic puddle of emotions sometimes.)

Once again I internalized the admittedly somewhat idealistic notions I've always had for my family and found myself preparing a mental checklist of things to do, to appreciate, to encourage, and to embrace with Rick, Kristen, Ricky Neal, and Patrick. It's what I want us all to do, to a healthy degree, as One Tough Mothers who are truly, madly, and deeply determined to get all they can out of their incredible family.

I want us to purposely pursue a crazy, one-of-a-kind appreciation for our children and spouses.

I want us to intentionally create moments of family connection which will sear indelible memories upon the hearts of our children, our spouses, and ourselves.

I want us to establish and articulate core relational values that define who we are corporately as a family.

And I want us to love and laugh and be goofy and be different and revel in the unique beauty of being family—my family—your family. Each one is unlike any other human unit of personalities, temperaments, strengths, and weaknesses upon the face of the planet—past, present, or future.

The following pages offer a host of ideas to jump-start your own truly, madly, deeply mothering. Some have been tested and approved over time with my own family. Others were sent to me by readers, event attendees, and friends and family via email and handwritten letters, while a couple I simply picked up from a well-written sitcom.

As always, they are here for your consideration, use, and enjoyment. Take what you want. Leave what you don't. But incorporate at least one into your family before you go to bed today. It's not brain surgery or rocket science;

it's simply creating, shaping, and enjoying the truly, madly, deeply beauty of your individual family.

# You Are What You Believe

Dr. James MacDonald, a pastor and author I have come to highly respect, spoke of his family's core values on an audio CD:

> Choose family values and post them at home. When we moved into our home we had our family values painted on our living room wall where our whole family can see them. These are ours—you can write and post your own:
>
> > *Love God.* How straight up is that? Right? Big surprise. What is the greatest commandment? *Love the Lord your God with all your heart.*
> > *Family first.* "Don't talk to your sister like that." "That's your mother!" "We are together in this." Loyalty. Family first.
> > *Work hard.* "This is your home, too. Put in the extra effort."
> > *Tell the truth.* Even when it's hard. Even when it's going to get you into more trouble. Just get the truth on the table. God can do a lot with that.
> > *Be kind.* "We are not going to talk about them like that. That is not kind."[1]

Well, I can't say I'm ready to paint our list on the wall of our house quite yet (it's substantially longer and would take quite a bit of space), but I have made a concerted effort over the years to say them over and over again, have asked the children to repeat them back to me, and to the best of my ability have lived them out in my own life. Here they are:

Respect authority—God, parents, other adults, police, teachers

Be tenderhearted—toward those who are overlooked

Know the Bible—and trust in its truths

Love on each other—show outward expressions of love—verbally, physically, and through actions of service to and for one another

Rest in love—be secure in the love of Rick and me for one another and toward them

Laugh whenever possible

Be one another's cheerleader—stand by and stand up for one another as siblings

Speak truth

Do well the first time

Get it done—stick with a job, sport, or commitment until it's done—NO slacking off or quitting

I didn't know it at the time, but when I wrote those values out in longhand I was stating quite succinctly what I believed in, what really mattered to me, and what values I believed important enough to live, demonstrate, and pass on not only to my children but to my children's children. I've often believed a new golden rule should be set forth declaring, "Do unto your children as you would have them do unto your grandchildren."

You see, moms, that's exactly what we're doing when we establish and live out core values specific to our family's life and future. We're intentionally and purposefully leaving a legacy of grace and faith for decades and centuries to come. How amazing when we think of it in such generational light! That's why this is a One Tough Mother nonnegotiable; it not only impacts our immediate family but also sets in motion wonderful things for those yet to be born.

# A Barnhill Always . . . : Identifying Family Distinctives

This tracks with our core values but helps broaden the truly, madly, deeply perspective of our individual family. What I'd like you to do is to consider one of your core values (example: showing tenderheartedness for those who are often overlooked) and then apply tangible, workable proofs of that value—workable proofs that can become distinctive characteristics collectively for your family and for each one individually. For example, I want my children not only to *feel* tenderhearted toward those who are often overlooked; I want them to *see* and to *engage* those who are overlooked. Thus a common statement in our family is, "A Barnhill always looks for the one person least expecting to be noticed in a crowded room." And when we spy that person? Well, we walk toward them, ask them their name, and do what we talkative Barnhills do.

Other inclusive mottos include,

"A Barnhill always gives the benefit of the doubt."
"A Barnhill always gives a little more." (This is generally spoken by me when filling up glasses of chocolate milk or dispensing portions of a favorite dessert.)
"A Barnhill's last words out the door are words he or she can live at peace with."

What motto could you claim for your family?

# Treasured Traditions

A close friend of mine creates with her family what she refers to as a "thankful tree" each Thanksgiving season. Emails and letters are sent to hundreds of friends across the world requesting the recipient respond by listing something they have been most grateful for over the past year. Each response is then written upon a cut-out leaf and adhered to a six-foot rendition of, well, a thankful tree. Ellie and her family have done this for years, and one of her five children living at home is always sure to remind her lest she somehow forget to send those emails and letters out for material. What a wonderful way to maintain a strong family tradition within your own ranks as well as honor the manifold blessings of others in the process.

Truly, madly, deeply traditions are so important in families—the sense of security and love that is felt when observing traditions as a family will stay with our children for the rest of their lives.

### Woo-Woo Hanky Wave!

One family always carries a set of white hankies with them to any and all events featuring members of their family. This includes sporting events, musical recitals, golf tournaments, cooking contests, swim meets, and Bible memorization speed drills at their local church. Nothing is considered off-limits with this raucous group of brothers and sisters, mother and dad. As you can probably guess, the point is to cheer and shout and animatedly "woo-woo" hanky wave their own to a first or even last place finish. The winning doesn't matter so much as the supporting one another (and yes, perhaps even good-naturedly embarrassing one of the more introspective family members).

### Red Plate Special

I purchased one of those "You Are Special" plates about seven years ago, but instead of waiting for once a year or once in a lifetime happenings such as birthdays or a report card filled with straight A's, I routinely get it down and serve up a favorite meal just because. Invariably one of the children asks, "What's so special about him or her?" I absolutely love this, for it then gives me the opportunity to implement another truly, madly, deeply mom thing . . . that of making, yes, making the children tell the red-plate person what is indeed special about them. (The teenagers especially love this!) Granted, one has to monitor forthcoming comments at times, but once we get past a few smart-aleck jabs, it generally turns into a fairly decent love-fest. Well, okay, maybe not. But at least the sibling gets to hear their brother and sister say something other than, "You're a complete idiot."

## O Christmas Tree, O Christmas Tree

My mother had an artificial Christmas tree that I always thought was gorgeous when I was a kid. But at some point (I believe it was somewhere around my sixteenth birthday) I decided just about everything my mother did was wrong and came to the conclusion she was somehow limiting the quality of my holiday experience by not allowing a real tree to enter our home. Then and there I vowed that when I became a mother, my children would *always* have a real Christmas tree. (Heaven help all readers parenting a sixteen-year-old child!)

Well, I kept my vow. We've had a real tree displayed in our living room since 1987, and the process for getting it there hasn't varied too far from one particular memory back in the nineties. It goes something like this . . .

The entire family holiday "finding a perfect Christmas tree" experience is supposed to resemble a Norman Rockwell moment with a bit of Thomas Kinkade thrown in for good measure. (Am I the only woman who wishes that man would quit painting all those pictures of light? I mean, come on, not one burned-out bulb in sight, how unrealistic is that?) The perfect experience also requires traveling to a locally owned tree farm where warm cocoa and snickerdoodles await those shopping for a tree. At least that's what my family was expecting when we went shopping for our tree for Christmas 1997.

So we made our way to the local tree farm, ate cookies, drank cocoa, and then waited as the female owner handed us a cute little hacksaw and two-by-two kneeling mat to use for felling the perfect Barnhill Christmas tree.

"Oh, look!" I exclaimed to eight-year-old Kristen and six-year-old Ricky. "You both get to use this to help Daddy cut down the perfect tree for our house. And after you help cut it down, we'll carry it back to the office, get it wrapped with netting, and then put it on the truck and take it home with us—isn't this exciting, you guys?"

They each crammed another snickerdoodle in their mouth, smiled, and nodded at their crazy mom. Then we began to walk . . . and walk . . . and walk. All through the farm—looking at trees, approximating the height of trees, rejecting trees—oh, and did I mention it was nearly twenty degrees below zero (okay, maybe I exaggerate just a tad but it was a typical Illinois late December afternoon—hence, cold) and the fact that neither of my older children had chosen to wear stocking caps or gloves? So there we were with the wind blowing, trudging through snow as high as our thighs, with Patrick's cheeks the color of Rudolph's glowing nose, when we finally agreed on a tree. More accurately told, Rick put his foot down and said, "That's it, I'm not walking any further, and it's this one or nothing."

Throwing the mat down, Rick then allowed Ricky Neal to begin cutting the trunk as he had been begging and pleading to do for the past six months and all the time we were wading through snowbanks. He knelt, drew the saw once, then twice, across the bark and then whined, "I'm tired. I don't wanna do this anymore." Kristen gave it her best shot and then joined Ricky Neal's chorus of, "I'm cold, my cheeks hurt, and I want more cookies." Inject movie soundtrack of *Psycho* as Crazy Mom responds, "Well, you should have worn your hat and gloves like I told you, shouldn't you? Now be quiet, we're cutting the tree."

So my husband got on his knees and started sawing and sawing while sticky, piney tree gunk adhered to his head of hair and jacketed body, each sawing motion loosening dead pine needles which then covered him from head to toe. Finally the tree fell and the children and I walked ahead of Rick as he muttered incoherently and dragged the perfect Barnhill Christmas tree back to be wrapped and loaded.

At last we left, the five of us stuffed into a Toyota pickup built for three with a pine tree precariously tied to the roof. Cautiously Rick made his way home, all the while explaining to the older children, "Okay, when we get home it's very important we slowly and *gently* remove the netting around the tree and allow plenty of time for the branches to warm up and fall into place. Don't forget that, kids—we'll slowly and gently allow the branches to fall, and then we'll decorate our tree."

Before too long we arrived home, brought the tree into the living room, set it into the tree stand, and tightened the screws until it stood perfectly straight. Rick and I were standing back and admiring our work when out of nowhere Ricky Neal appeared with a set of scissors and faster than you could say "Didn't-hear-a-thing-his-father-said-in-the-truck-about-slowly-and-gently-removing-the-netting," the branches violently burst free from their binding and nearly sent him flying through a plate glass window. Okay, another slight exaggeration, but those branches did some serious bursting free, and the aftermath revealed piney branch scratches on Ricky's disobedient face. His father and I had a difficult time feeling sorry for him in the least.

At this point we were both too frustrated to wait for the lowering of the limbs, so we decided to go ahead and decorate the tree.

Sigh.

This would, of course, involve each of the children, and Patrick was approximately three feet tall that year. He insisted on helping and zealously placed ornament after ornament after ornament on the not-so-relaxed tree branches with his chubby little toddler hands. He was so proud of himself, and a good mom doesn't go back and redo her child's handiwork, right? So we had six hundred ornaments all nestled together on the lower one-quarter quadrant.

It was, without a doubt, the ugliest Christmas tree I had ever seen.

And then it was time for the grand finale: the lowering of the angel.

Each year we allowed a different child the honor; however, we had failed to write down whose turn it was, and so Kristen and Ricky Neal began to speak to one another in the love language known to all siblings:

"You big dummy, it's my turn to put the angel on top!"

"No, it isn't, you got to do it last year and you stunk at it!"

"I did not, and you're stupid!"

One comment after another until my sweet, easygoing husband had heard all he could take and bellowed so loud the windows nearly shook, "That's it! That's it! I've had enough of both of you! Get upstairs, go to your rooms, and don't come out until I tell you to—*I'm* going to put the angel on the tree!"

And all the while Amy Grant was singing in the background.

(Oh, come on! You know what I'm writing about.)

Okay, we've haven't always handled holiday details in the healthiest of truly, madly, deeply ways, but if nothing else we're consistent in our trying to do something unique and thoroughly Barnhill. Plus, they always make for wonderful stories later on down the road.

Choosing what is important for your family is the main thing. Maybe you bake a specific dish or decorate each room of the house in a thoroughly unique manner. The possibilities are limited only by your imagination. Be it *Southern Living* style or something akin to a *National Lampoon's Christmas Vacation*—be there to create, encourage, and enjoy what makes the holidays special and memorable for those you love.

Core values. Family mottos. Treasured traditions. Each of these will water the seeds of that truly, madly, deeply love One Tough Mother has for her family.

# 9

# These Things I Know to Be True

## Nonnegotiable #7: Remember It's All Worth It

In the spring of 2006, I was a keynote speaker for the Hearts at Home national conference held on the campus of Illinois State University. I had been a first-time mom attendee thirteen years before (and consistently made my way back thereafter) and was delighted to find myself center stage all those years later—hoping to give back just a small portion of the encouragement and insight other speakers and workshop leaders had poured into my life when I was a young and then increasingly older mom of three children.

Over the course of the months leading up to the conference, I began to think about what I would actually speak about. After all, by the time the women made their way to the comfy seats of Braden Auditorium for an afternoon session with me, they would have listened to three or four workshop sessions as well as a morning keynote with Hearts at Home's founder and director, Jill Savage.

In all likelihood every emotional heartstring would have been tugged, every conference journal page would be filled with notes on insights and "aha!" moments, and information overload would be threatening to shut down their brains and eyelids.

Trust me, that afternoon session can be a killer. I knew my message needed to explode with energy, humor, and, well, substance, so I simply asked myself, "Julie, after nearly twenty years of being a mom, what do you know is true?" It didn't take long to come up with a list.

I know a nauseated child will always come to his or her mother's side of the bed. It's written in stone or on some ancient papyrus, a childhood commandment of sorts: "Thou shalt lean thyself over thy mother's groggy face anytime after 12:54 a.m. and pronounce the likelihood of thou upchucking upon her."

I know this to be true.

But let me add a bigger truth to this one: if you are the mother of more than one child, the manner in which you handle the situation will alter greatly between children.

When it was just my firstborn, Kristen, toddling into my room and threatening to hurl one hundred of the three hundred Cheerios she had consumed that day, I was patient, long-suffering, and oh so verbally gentle and kind.

"Kristen, sweetie, Mommy's here," I would say as I scooped her up with nary a concern regarding the silky satin nightgown I was wearing and gently cupped a hand beneath her mouth just in case we failed to make it to the bathroom. I would then sit near her, gently wiping her forehead with a cool rag and bravely managing to not get sick at the sight and sound of her getting sick. (I have an embarrassingly weak stomach for being One Tough Mother.)

Now, when the situation involved her brother Ricky Neal, the scenario shifted just a bit. Ricky Neal never toddled into any room. Not once. Not ever. His forward button was set on "barrel and bulldoze" from the moment of his conception. So when he charged into the bedroom and hovered one-and-a-quarter inches from my face, I would jump out of bed, hold him football style with his mouth turned away from my tattered, paper-thin, Garfield the Cat nightshirt, and make a mad dash for the bathroom, all the while saying, "Try not to throw up on Mommy!"

And then there was Patrick.

Poor Patrick.

Green at the gills, he would come to our room, make his way to my side of the bed, and then attempt to wake his mother (who was sleeping like the dead) with a mannerly finger poke and persistent, "Momma, Momma, Momma, Momma . . ." Over and over and over again. And I would hear him, truly I would, but part of me hoped against hope that he would move on to his daddy.

"Momma, Momma, Momma, Momma . . ."

After the 103rd "Momma," I would haul my thirty-some-thing-year-old flannel pants and Johnny Bravo T-shirted body out of bed, take him by the hand, lead him back to his room, and say, "Patrick, Momma's going to put your St. Louis Rams football trash can right here next to your bed. If you think you have to get sick, just lean your head over the can and yell for Daddy."

Poor, poor, Patrick.

I know this to be true.

I also know that the free measuring cup you picked up at a Tupperware party at Barb Storm's house in 1992 will cost you exactly $276.49 in 1998 to extract from a downstairs toilet after being flushed by the aforementioned third child.

I know the laser thing in automatic paper towel dispensers in most malls and department stores is right about the height of a three-year-old kid. And if that kid stands in front and moves his head back and forth over and over again, piles of paper will accumulate in the wake of toddler giggles and irritated mom's commands to "Stop it!"

I know a Cocoa Puff embedded in the left nostril is nearly impossible to extract.*

I know if a child of mine is going to throw up on my best friend's new carpeting (Sandy Beach White), it will only be after consuming a full two liters of Razzle-Dazzle Raspberry Kool-Aid.

*It was only during the editing process of writing that I learned the Secret to aforementioned dilemma: Crush and blow!

And here's a truth too fun to forget: I know that if you want to totally freak out your teenager, you need only imply in any way whatsoever that you are a sexual being. (Oh, I'm laughing as I write this! Any implication at all just puts them over the edge, you see. After all, we're asexual cyborgs or something to them.)

Here's a perfect example—feel free to follow in my steps.

Last Christmas Rick and I sat around a dining room table playing the game Taboo with my brother- and sister-in-law Rod and Dona and our five combined children: Kristen, Brett, Ricky Neal, Corey, and Patrick.

I don't much like board games of any sort, but Taboo is largely made up of words, and since I love to use words and learn new ones, I like Taboo. So there we all sat and played, just like a Norman Rockwell painting. Suddenly it was Rick's turn to describe the word he wanted his team to say. And by the way, his team consisted of Ricky Neal, our nephew Corey, and Patrick.

So the timekeeper turned the one-minute timer over, and my man sounded something like this:

"Umm, this is, uh, something I'd really like to see your mom wear to bed instead of the bleach-dotted, paint-splattered, awful Johnny Bravo T-shirt she has worn since 1999 . . . Let's see . . . It's soft and satiny and can be purchased at Wal-Mart or Victoria's Secret, since your mother always likes to pay more than she has to for clothing."

And all the while the kids, my sons in particular, are staring at him like he's speaking Chinese or something. With seconds remaining in the minute, he continues, "Lots of women like your mom wear these when they're first married and their husbands really, really, really like it and wish they would continue to do s—"

Time was up and the kids didn't have a clue.

None whatsoever.

But I did, and I couldn't wait until they heard it.

"Geesh, Dad, what was the word?" Patrick asked.

"Yeah," said Ricky Neal, "I don't have a clue what you were trying to describe."

Smiling from ear to ear and raising his eyebrows in a hubba-hubba manner, Rick then sloooowly turned the card around and said, "Negligee"—with a bit too much enthusiasm for his children.

"Oh! Now that's just flat-out disturbing," Ricky Neal declared with disgust. Patrick, who looked like he could have used that St. Louis Rams trash can right about then, dropped his head and muttered, "That's sick, Dad, totally sick."

I'm talking full-body shudders and plaintive wails of "Guh-ross!" and "That's just not right!" I took their comments a bit personally and said somewhat defensively, "Hey! There *are* worse things than me in a negligee! Trust me, I saw my grandma in her underwear once."

Rick and I were laughing so hard we snorted. It was priceless.

Sometimes it's just too easy, you know what I mean?

Here's another thing I know to be true: there are things about motherhood that no one could have ever properly prepared you for even if they had tried.

But you know what? It's all worth it. Because for every midnight dash to the bathroom and three-hundred-dollar "free measuring cup" extraction there's a fun night of family games (and shameless embarrassment of your teen!) to bring the kind of laughter and comfort that remind you it's all worth it.

That's the truth I know above all others: this is all worth it.

Remembering that truth isn't always easy in the midst of the tough moments, days, and years of motherhood. But if you take the time to cultivate two things—laughter and comfort—in the midst of it all, you'll remember this worth-it-all truth at the end of the day.

## Laughter Is the Best Medicine

I have said things, done things, believed things, and put my kids up to things that sent me sprawling to the ground in laughter. And I don't regret any of it.

If there is any area of being One Tough Mother that I feel I have figured out more than another, it is this area of seizing the fun of life and trying to never pass up an opportunity to laugh with my kids. It's always been important to me to cultivate humor in my own home, for it's tethered to what I have referred to in other writings as my "in the light of eternity" mission statement: *In the light of eternity, I want my adult children to choose to return home.*

In the light of eternity, I want my adult children to be able to sit around and recall memory after memory of "laughing our heads off that day in the living room" or "always knowing Mom was going to find something funny in everything." (And, yes, you'd be correct in diagnosing my need to *control* things as one of my chief problems as a mom!)

Growing up in my childhood home, I heard few outbursts of laughter. My father could appreciate a good joke, but he never would have been mistaken for Billy Crystal. And my mom, well, my mom was often as much an enigma to me as I was to her. She listened to my silly stories and would chuckle occasionally at my jokes, but I rarely, if ever, heard her let loose with a bodacious roar of laughter. My parents were (and still are) far more reserved than I ever was or ever will be.

But I managed to have a marvelous childhood anyway and determined early on to create an environment of raucous fun and entertainment in my own future family life. And that's pretty much what I've done. (But I do find it interesting that I married a rather reserved man. Go figure.)

From my children's earliest years, I instilled within them an appreciation for comedic timing, the power of a well-delivered line, and the sheer thrill of basking in the sound of laughter.

I've heard more bad knock-knock jokes than you can even imagine.

There isn't a *Good Clean Joke Book* that hasn't been quoted to me over and over and over again.

And nobody does plain old stupid jokes better than the Barnhills.

I believe each one of us as moms can and needs to purposefully weave a thread of intentional fun, laughter, and joy throughout the lives and experiences of our families if we're to keep sight of that "it's all worth it" truth. I also believe a foundational part of learning to be the mom in this area involves taking into careful account the unique personalities and dynamics of each child and parent within the home.

It's very important you not try to mimic my or any other author's examples to a T. That's not the point. Rather, I desire for each of you to gain motivational support and inspiration to do what best suits your family. Be the mom with the talents and abilities you have when it comes to this area, and as you begin to incorporate some of the following threads, weave them in such a manner as to best create an atmosphere of contagious joy and laughter with your children and as a family.

### Movie Quotes to Last a Laughtime

(Sorry, I couldn't let that pun pass.)

Some of our best moments of connecting as a family have been the direct result of wonderful movie quotes. Now, I realize some of you may be anti-Hollywood, or anti–implied cartoon mischief, or anti–anything other than Narnia, and I want you to know I'm not here to knock what you believe or to try to convert you to my line of thinking.

After all, I was the lone mother who would not allow her five-year-old kindergartener to watch *Pocahontas* during movie week. (That was during my One Tough Mother anti-pantheism and anti-naturalism stage of spiritual development.) I've had more than a couple of times in my role as mother when I all but chucked the television and DVD player entirely. But I'm kinda shallow, if you must know, and I just haven't ever been willing to give up my FOX News, *Cold Case Files*, and *What Not to Wear* or the liberty of watching *The Princess Bride* for the one thousandth time.

Trust me on this, moms: having a bank of quotes that you and your children have compiled over time can be a hilarious way of strengthening your relationship and adding humorous punch to what would otherwise be an ordinary moment.

For instance, one Sunday my family and I were all packed into a church pew, listening to the morning sermon. It had something to do with King Herod being anything but a nice and friendly tyrant and his seeming ability to see and hear everything that was going on under his rule. Truth be told, I was mostly listening until my eyes were suddenly drawn to the PowerPoint image on the gigantic screen above Pastor Kirk's head.

There, in living Pixar color, was a shot of Roz—an unforgettable character in the animated movie *Monsters, Inc.* Within seconds of her image hitting the screen, Ricky Neal and I both leaned forward, turned to face one another from opposite ends of the row, and silently mouthed, "I'm watching you, Wazowski. Always watching."

Oh. My. Goodness!

I don't think I've ever suppressed a snort like I did that morning.

We timed it perfectly.

The *lean*,
    the eye contact,
        and the quote.

I thought we were both going to blow a gasket as we leaned back and attempted to control our laughter. It wasn't easy. And it was probably quite obvious to those seated right behind me that something was amiss. We were both attempting to do the "silent church laugh" thing.

Eyes looking downward at our feet.

Arms to our sides.

While our shoulders reverberated with pent-up laughter.

What a hoot! An otherwise staid and bland PowerPoint moment enhanced by a thread of humor. See, Ricky Neal and I had watched *Monsters, Inc.* time and time again when he was younger. He had a natural affinity for accents and verbal inflections and early on began to mimic any unusual or comedic voices in movies. Roz was one of those characters. And there we were, four or five years down the movie road, when my son and I were able to find a comedic connection with one another. I can't think of a better place to share a silent laugh with my child.

It doesn't get any better than that, moms.

Other timeless movies that are sure to stimulate your funny bone include the 1967 children's classic *The Jungle Book* and anything remotely related to a Pooh bear. I danced and jiggled my, um, shoulders and sang, "I wanna be like you-ooo-ooo," Baloo-the-bear-style a hundred if not a thousand times with all my children. Once when Patrick had his feelings hurt by a friend, Kristen put her arm around his shoulder and began to sing, "We're your friends," a la the vulture. Now that's got warm and fuzzy written all over it!

And who can't appreciate and love the antics of that tubby little cubby all stuffed with fluff? On days my children turned sullen or solemn I would try to pull them out of their doldrums via an Eeyore conversation or singing the Tigger song. It always helped to bounce on one leg when belting out, "The wonderful thing about Tiggers, is Tiggers are wonderful things. Their tops are made out of rubber; their bottoms are made out of springs."

It makes me laugh and sing even as I write!

Each of us can purposely build a library of quotes and songs and memories to enhance the fun factor in our homes. Everyone will take a different route to this, and there isn't a particular right way to go about it. Simply keep an eye and ear open to any and all possibilities. Perhaps it will be a golden oldie—or a newer release such as *Finding Nemo* (and no, this is not a paid endorsement for a certain movie mogul empire!). Whether it's old or new, faith-based or just good clean family entertainment, you'll never regret shoring up your comedic reserves. The dividends will last a lifetime.

## Annoyingly Funny Songs That Get Stuck in Your Head

"Oh, where is my hairbrush? Oh, where is my hairbrush? Oh . . ." Sing it with me, girls, before I run out of copyright leeway!

Have any more annoyingly funny songs come down the musical pipeline than those produced by the writers of VeggieTales? I don't think so! So I urge you with the strongest of "be the mom!" urges to pick up a copy or two of the *Silly Songs* soundtracks and water buffalo your way to giggles galore. Memorize the lines of "I Love My Lips" and impress your children's friends (and horrify your teenagers) by belting out a refrain or two while driving down the road or baking cookies in the kitchen.

And when you've worn out your lyrical welcome, you can always pop in a copy of a VeggieTales movie and come up with a whole host of obnoxiously appealing quotes and sound bites. My personal favorite in the VeggieTales movie category comes from *Josh and the Big Wall* when a character asks, "How are we clappin', we ain't got no hands?" (The characters are, after all, just a bunch of appendage-free vegetables.)

Splendid, I tell you. Absolutely splendid.

## "185"

A lot of times we have only two options: laugh or curl up into a fetal position and cry. Another great way of promoting laughter is to play "185."

As my children have grown older, it truly has been necessary for me to diligently create and look for opportune moments for family laughter. I noticed some time ago that we were falling into the monotonous and brain-numbing drill of eating dinner while watching television and then staring at the screen with little or no verbal interaction other than, "Hey! Turn back to the baseball game," or "No, you cannot watch *Paris Hilton's Guide to the Sweet Life!*"

Now, prior to this observation, Rick and I had attended an employee recognition party, which he, as human resource director, had been in charge of planning. The entertainment he had chosen for the night was phenomenal! Comedy-Sportz, an improvisational comedy troupe involving a whole group of performers making up scenes and playing games on the spot based on audience suggestions, kept everyone on their toes and laughing and begging for more.

I couldn't get enough of it and practically had to be tied down as I so badly wanted to get up on stage and give it my best improv shot. Throughout the ride home Rick and I kept talking about how entertaining (and clean!) it had all been.

So fast-forward back to our living room and its dull atmosphere.

Grabbing the remote control, I shut off the television and announced to the kids, "Hey! Your dad and I learned a great game of sorts when we went out the other night, and we're going to teach it to you."

The children were thrilled. Really. Just thrilled.

*Teetotalers may replace "bar" with "store" and "bartender" with "store manager."

Moving forward, I then explained, "Okay, what I want us to do is play the '185' game. What you're going to do is name three in-animate objects, and I will then use one to complete the following phrase: 185 _____ walked into a bar.* The bartender says, 'I'm sorry, but we don't serve _____ in here.' And the _____ replied, '_____.' So shout out three non-living, non-breathing objects."

All three children stared at me briefly, but they're no longer surprised in the least when their mother comes up with something like they had just heard. So they humored me and named the following: garbage cans, bras, and ticks. And I got to work. Here's how it went:

"Okay . . . 185 bras walked into a bar, and the bartender said, 'I'm sorry, we don't serve bras in here.' The 185 bras replied, 'Ah, man, we brought our own cups!"

They smirked and I knew I had 'em.

So for the following sixty minutes or more, we all sat in the living room creating pun after pathetic pun. And here's what was most delightful about the entire thing, moms: we were able to wallow in the goofiness of our differences and laugh and groan with and for one another as we all attempted to top the others and hit one out of the improv park.

The kids delighted in watching their father try his best to come up with something witty (it takes him a bit longer than me, but when he does it, he really does it well) and soon began to cheer for one another as they gained more and more confidence in pun making.

This is so much fun, and here's why: it's goofy, it's inane, and it makes no sense. Your kids will love it for the goofy and senseless factors. You'll love it because it will give you an opportunity to see the personality dynamics of you and your children in all their glory. See, every family is made up of quick-witted members as well as those more prone to pondering.

Ricky Neal and I—and Patrick too, more and more—are lightning fast in our thoughts and responses. Rick and Kristen, well, not so much. They mull over their thoughts. They ponder their puns. And they are hilarious to watch and listen to while doing so. The "185" game is not about laughing at one another but about laughing with each other and appreciating what makes us each so darn unique and different.

My husband is like Halley's Comet. Rick says something phenomenally funny about once every seventy-six years.

Meanwhile, Ricky Neal's mouth can't keep up with his clever thoughts.

Kristen looks a lot like Rodin's *The Thinker* when playing.

And Patrick laughs at just about everything anybody says and comes up with puns far beyond what I would have imagined him creating.

We've played this game for hours, and it isn't uncommon now for one of us to randomly insert a "185" thought while driving across town to Ludlum's Grocery Mart.

Listen, you One Tough Mother, you: we have to have laughter to keep us sane and to keep us normal and to keep us from taking ourselves all too seriously. But you and I both know it's one of the first things to go (right after The Girls heading south). You push that baby out or sign the final paper for adoption, and the powers that be require the handing over of your laughter, sense of humor, and ability to laugh at yourself—thank you very much.

But we have to take that back!

I want to encourage you with every funny One Tough Mother fiber within me to pursue laughter and the eternal benefits of a merry heart.

No doubt about it, laughter is a thread woven into the very construct of our home. A day without laughter is a day sadly wasted in my book, so it probably doesn't come as much of a surprise that I have purposefully and tenaciously pursued adding it to my children's lives throughout the past two decades.

This is why every moment you seize matters, moms.

# My Home as a Sanctuary of Healing, Security, and Rest

Within the next twenty-four hours, make your way to your nearest Box-Mart shopping emporium or local grocery store and purchase the biggest box of all-purpose Band-Aids you can possibly buy. It's very important the box reads "all-purpose," for I want you to buy those Band-Aids and then go home, get out a stout Sharpie marker, put a big X through the word *all*, and write in its place the word *no*, as in "NO-purpose Band-Aids."

Do this and place them with your other medical supplies.

Then the next time a young child (yours, a sibling's, or perhaps even a neighbor's) performs a dramatic, over-the-top, Oscar award–winning, "I'm really milking this for all it's worth" crying jag over a miniscule scrape or boo-boo and everything in you wants to just look at it and declare, "Are you kidding me? You think this deserves a Band-Aid?"—I want you to think of what is true instead.

Stop and think of your home as a haven of healing to all those who enter its doors or cross its yard. Think of creating a haven of security and rest and instead of belittling a little one's grandiose concept of pain, reach instead for that box of "no-purpose" Band-Aids. In fact, reach for and grab two or three of those no-purpose Band-Aids, and then gently and lovingly place each one near the wound site.

Here's a One Tough Mother truth: no wound in a family is so small as to be overlooked. How little effort it takes to close our mouth and reach for a Band-Aid. And what a rich reward for those of us who choose to create a haven of healing, a place where injuries (physical, emotional, sexual, and spiritual) are cared for and lovingly ministered to. What juxtaposition with the home where wounds are inflicted. May it never be said of us as One Tough Mothers!

Some of you reading these pages may be struggling with that very reality even today. You have inflicted some wounds in your home. Words have been spoken that you would take back a million times if it were only possible. Thoughts have run rampant that left you feeling miserable and guilty. Perhaps you have acted out in anger, or shut yourself down emotionally, or done or said or thought a thousand and one things that you wish could be undone.

Here's what I'd like you to do: grab that same box of Band-Aids again, remove a handful, and then go to that child you have hurt, peel the backing from the Band-Aid, and place the bandage on the portion of their body you have hurt. Perhaps you spewed unkind and unprovoked words—gently stick a small one on their earlobe and one near their heart and tell them, "Mommy realizes she has said words that hurt your ears and heart, and I want you to know I'm sorry. So I'm going to put this Band-Aid over your heart, for I know it has hurt from my words, and this one I'm going to stick on your adorable earlobe, for I know your ears have stung from my angry words. I love you, and I want our home to be a place where you feel and know you are safe—this is my way of saying I'm sorry and to let you know I'm going to start speaking words that heal your heart rather than hurt it."

If you know you have over-spanked your child or perhaps handled them roughly in public due to your own frustration, embarrassment, or childishness, I encourage you to do the same thing. A child is never too young and never too old to hear their mother say, "I was wrong. I hurt you. I'm sorry."

We also create a haven—a sanctuary in our homes—with our choice of fabrics and wall colors. A couple of years ago I painted our living room with faux suede paint and created a rich, brushed look that begged visitors to nestle in deep amongst chenille throws and baby-soft pillows punctuating the sofa. I heard so many compliments that I did the same wall treatment in my dining room four days before I was to host Thanksgiving dinner for nearly twenty people. It took nearly fourteen hours from start to finish, but the gorgeous wine-berry-colored walls made it all worth it.

You don't have to spend an outrageous amount of money to create a sense of security and warmth. Go to your nearest dollar store and pick up a package of tea lights. Place them around your rooms and create an ambiance with their low, flickering light (for those with little ones, this idea may have to wait a bit, or you may find it necessary to purchase some very inexpensive shelving upon which you can safely rest a burning light).

Pick up some soft throws to snuggle up with on cool nights.

Purchase small mirrors, place candles on them, and enjoy the reflections.

Play music that settles the soul rather than setting it on edge.

Bake a batch of cookies for the aromatic welcome.

Goodness knows you'll find a plethora of magazines, decorating experts, and TLC programming to help you along the way. I know this much to be true: it's worth every moment you spend in creating an emotional and physical haven for you and your family.

I consider how each one of my children has fit into the sanctuary of my heart. Kristen is the thinker of our family, melancholy in nature and, according to a couple of books I've read about temperaments, prone to being a genius. I don't doubt this fact, as this was the two-year-old child who gazed upon a full moon and repeatedly identified it as "Ball, ball, ball." This is the same child who folded up her socks and lined them up neatly in a dresser drawer as a six-year-old.

I refer to her as a thinker because she is prone to analytical thought and seldom takes anything (or anyone) merely at face value. I could pull one over on Ricky Neal and even Patrick, but Kristen? No, Kristen generally carries an "Uh-huh, we'll see about that" air about her.

If I had just had Kristen, I probably wouldn't be writing this book. Better said, perhaps, if I had just had Kristen, you probably wouldn't want to read this book. My expert One Tough Mother advice would have sounded more than a little pompous and sure. Don't do this or that. By all means, do this exactly the way I did it.

I would have dictated two, maybe three bada-bing, bada-bang enunciations from the heavenly realm of immaculate perfection mothering. And you would have wanted to pop my head off like a Pez candy dispenser.

But none of that happened, because I had Ricky Neal.

And Ricky Neal obliterated any and all "I've got this all figured out" thoughts and gloating. Extroverted, rambunctious, and frightfully fearless, Ricky Neal never met a dresser drawer he didn't love to upend on a bedroom floor or a rock cliff he didn't want to scale and then plummet from. I had no expert One Tough Mother advice to write or speak during this child's early years, for my brain was fried and my time was spent journaling harried notes such as, "I don't have a clue what I'm doing!" He is the polar opposite of his older sister and was our lone form of birth control for nearly four years.

Then there was Patrick.

He was quite possibly the most beautiful baby ever born. His impossibly round shaped skull—despite his being nine pounds and eleven ounces at birth and requiring nearly an hour of impossibly hard pushing to deliver—coupled with his deep brown eyes the size of quarters all but screamed,

"Look at me! I'm the most adorable boy on the face of the earth." Gregarious like his brother, a reader like his sister, Patrick rounded out, wrapped up, and settled once and for all what I believed to be true for my family and perhaps yours too.

It's the nonnegotiable truth I want you to take with you forever. (How's that for wanting to make an impact on your life?) I know how important laughter and security are in the lives of our children and for us as One Tough Mother, for I have lived it out—I've seen such truth lived out in my home and in the lives of my children, and I know each one strengthens and underscores every other nonnegotiable I have written in this book. And this I know to be true: it's worth all the effort and energy it takes to make laughter and security happen.

# 10

# Just Say It

## Nonnegotiable #8: Leave Nothing Unspoken

Time to get out of bed.

Go brush your teeth . . . again.

What do you want for breakfast?

Who put my bra on the dog?

Are you and your friends getting along better?

Please set the table for dinner.

Where's your tummy? Where's your nose? Good girl!

That's why I told you not to take milk into the living room in the first place!

Put gas in the Yukon this time or you won't be driving it again for a while.

Who got voted off *Idol*?

Please pass the mashed potatoes.

Sit still and quit pestering your sister.

Time to go night-night.

Would someone please bring me a roll of toilet paper!?

One hundred and eleven words; barely a dent in the near twenty thousand words many relationship experts say a woman will utter before her day is through. But what if the woman is a mom too? I did a fast survey online and flipped through some fact books from my library, but I couldn't find any estimates on the daily word count of someone like you or me—someone like One Tough Mother.

So I'm just going to make up my own statistic based on personal experience and twenty years of sitting around with other moms and listening as they've spoken to their children and told me about war stories from home. Based on those three factors, I'm going to guesstimate the average mother speaks no less than 35,000 words a day. Whew! That may sound crazy to the uninitiated (people without children), but you and I both know it's not all that difficult to do.

Before our feet even hit the floor, we're usually saying something to someone: "When did you climb into bed with Mommy?"

Before exiting the bathroom, we've usually engaged in lengthy discussions—not that anyone other than ourselves really cares or listens: "No, you can't come in while Mom is using the toilet. Gads, can't I have forty-three seconds of time to myself? Am I asking too much to simply be able to do what needs to be done without someone sticking their fingers under the door and squealing to come in or climbing on me while I sit and do my one-minute devotions or tripping me in the shower? Is that too much to ask? I don't think so!"

And we haven't even made it to the kitchen for our morning wake-up coffee or can of Pepsi.

As One Tough Mother, we find our life overflowing with thoughts and feelings. Thoughts and feelings, when expressed, have the power to encourage, rebuke, challenge, inspire, empower, and otherwise impact every aspect of our children's lives. (No pressure, right?)

I implied such a few chapters earlier when discussing a particular family distinctive: "A Barnhill's last words out the door are words he or she can live at peace with." I've drilled into my children (and husband) the truth that none of us should ever leave (or allow each other to leave) our house with an angry last word on their lips or an unspoken word that should have been said. Life is far too tenuous to do otherwise, for who among us knows what lies ahead in the next five minutes, hour, or year?

I don't really believe there is any reasonable excuse for any one of us leaving this world with words unspoken. We can always find time to make that call or pull a certain person aside and look them in the eye and say what needs to be said. To do otherwise is plain foolish.

I want my daughter and sons to hear from me—today, face-to-face, while we both are able to hug one another and speak one another's name.

I want your children to hear from you—today, face-to-face, while you both can revel in the sweetness and power of a well-appointed word.

Perhaps as painful and regretful as words we wish we could recall are those we wish we'd spoken. But it doesn't have to be that way, you know; One Tough Mother can wisely consider her days and purposely speak life and truth into the lives of her children. I believe our children need to hear several specifics first and foremost from us—their moms and biggest fans. As you read through them, please choose one—put down the book, even—and find your child and just say it.

# I'm So Glad I Had You!

Does anyone ever grow tired of hearing they are loved and cherished? I don't think anyone does, least of all our children. They're bottomless pits of "tell me how much you love me" enthusiasm and need. It's a good need, mind you, as their ever-developing perception of value and self-worth is tethered to the power of our spoken words regarding who they are and how we feel about them.

For close to ten years now, one of the things I've been instructing mothers to do is to pull their child away from the busyness of a given moment and find a quiet spot where the two of them can simply be. I encourage moms to then cup their child's face in the palms of their hands, look squarely into their eyes, beam with One Tough Mother pride, and firmly say, "I'm so glad I had you."

This is especially powerful when spoken to that certain child who often makes us want to run screaming through the house—powerful because it is spoken truth for both your hearts. Sure, some of our kids drive us bonkers. Some of our kids are very difficult to like. And some of our kids silently wonder if we've wished we'd never had them. (And while that thought probably has crossed your mind a time or two during difficult times, the truth is, you love your child and you are thankful for their creation and placement within your home.)

I especially make a point of routinely drawing Patrick aside and telling him, "I enjoy your company so much. I delight in your personality, and I am so happy God added you to our family right when he did." Patrick is twelve at the time of this writing, and he's a third child—hence the wisdom of my taking time to speak what needs to be spoken. Not tomorrow. Not when he's sixteen. But today.

# I Will Always Be Your Mom . . . No Matter What

Blah, blah, blah . . . or so it seems as these words seemingly pass through and fall on deaf ears. But trust me, they're listening! Oh, baby, are they ever listening.

Moms, don't ever stop speaking these words of truth. Start when they are babies and keep talking until you draw your last breath, for our children are taking it all in, and more than a few of them will call your hand as they stumble down the heartbreaking road of hard knocks and poor choices.

I know One Tough Mother whose four-year-old son pitches monstrous fits of frustration and screams out, "Go away, Mommy, I don't like you!" Her love? Steadfast and sure. Her status? Frazzled, but Mom nevertheless.

I know One Tough Mother whose teenage daughter has chosen to live a sexual lifestyle far removed from the dreams and moral beliefs of her mother. Her love? Steadfast and sure. Her status? Mom, always.

I know One Tough Mother whose son is serving a life sentence without the possibility of parole. His crime? Murder in the first degree. Her love? Unwavering. Her status? Steadfastly Mom.

Most of us will never know what it requires to visit our son in a maximum-security prison.

More than a few of us will contend with heartbreaking choices our teens and early adult children willfully yet foolishly make.

And nearly all of us will have a showdown with our own preschooler—and in all likelihood, it'll occur in a public forum.

There are no guarantees when it comes to raising children, are there? No magical checklist of do's and don'ts that we can log into an Excel spreadsheet and studiously monitor. Each of us is simply doing the best we know how and hopefully taking purposeful One Tough Mother steps toward understanding and change in areas we're not so sure about.

We love our children . . . no matter what. We just have to keep saying it today in order for them to believe it tomorrow.

# I'm Praying for You (Like It or Not)

You may recall a certain prayer regarding my daughter I cited in an early chapter of this book. It was 2003 and my petition sounded a little something, um, *exactly* like this: *"God! Help me figure out this child before I . . ."*

Up until my screaming cry for help, I had read all sorts of material about early teens and felt I had done a rather bang-up job of keeping the communication channels open as she entered adolescence and her freshman year of high school. I allowed her "her" space without feeling like I had taken my hands off the mothering reins completely (sigh . . . some of that all-powerful control stuff was creeping in around that time for sure). I kept ample supplies of Hot Pockets and chocolate chip cookie dough available for her friends and purposely brought her along for certain speaking events that I felt would enable her to meet other Christian girls and women who were plugged into a rich and dynamically rewarding faith.

But every day I felt I was losing her more and more.

I detected an unsettling callousness beginning to creep into her voice and gaze.

We argued over the typical things a hormonal daughter and equally hormonal mom do, but something was "not right"—that's the only way I can explain it, really. I just knew with One Tough Mother certainty that things were not as they should be.

Of course, my natural response was to talk it to death—with Kristen, with Rick, with my closest friends, with . . . well, just about anyone who would listen. But Kristen quickly shut me out. Rick grew frustrated with my need to examine the minutiae of every look and comment. And my friends could only do so much and listen so long. Quickly enough it was just me.

Well, me and God.

In a matter of a few months I came to the astounding conclusion that the single most important and effective thing I could do was pray for my daughter. Now, I'm not talking about some special kind of prayer that I had somehow missed all those years prior to 2003. No, my prayers had been quite consistent for her (and her brothers) for years; this was more of the "trust me with your child" type of praying which many of us get to after dealing with a malcontent for a long enough time.

And so I prayed.

But I went one step further: I stayed with this One Tough Mother nonnegotiable and I decided to tell Kristen exactly how I was going to be praying for her until the end of the world as we knew it. However, this time I chose to speak my words through the written page. I hoped she would tuck them within a dresser drawer or journal and be reminded of my love for her—and my commitment to her as her mother. Here's a few snippets of what I wrote:

> I pray that He would bless your heart. . . . I know you're trying to figure out what you believe. About God, sex, right, and wrong. About good things that happen. And evil things that seem to happen more than the good sometimes. Trying to figure it out isn't a bad thing. In fact, it's the very thing

that can make you a stronger thinker and a more committed individual. You're on a journey of faith as a young woman,

# Praying for Your Kids: 5 Easy Ways to Get Started

Author and speaker Susan Alexander Yates offers great advice for the mom who would like a little more direction when it comes to praying for her kids:

**Get Organized**—Use a notebook and divide it into seven sections, one for each day of the week. Choose a specific child or need to pray for on varying days. This way you won't feel like you have to remember everything and everybody every day.

**Ask What Your Child Needs**—Perhaps your elementary-school-aged daughter's struggling to find friends or your teen's questioning his faith. Ask God in the weeks ahead to reveal specific things you should be praying about for each of your children. If you're a single parent, do this with another mom or couple, and agree to pray for each other's children over the next several months.

**Use Prayers from Scripture**—When I don't know how to pray specifically for one of my children, I head directly to God's Word, which contains wonderful prayers. For example, Ephesians 1:17–19 is a beautiful prayer. So is Philippians 1:9–11. Insert your child's name into the prayer wherever it says "you."

**Expect God to Answer**—I've found his answers generally fall into one of three responses: "Yes," "No," or "Wait." If the answer is "wait," you may find yourself wondering if God hears or really cares. But God hears your prayers—and is at work in your child's life!

**Remember Who's in Control**—The task of praying for our kids can often overwhelm us. But don't forget, your children are God's children first. He knows them better than you do—and loves them more than you do. He also knows the plans he has prepared for them (Jeremiah 29:11). God's your partner in parenting; it's not all up to you.[1]

and it is a journey of great significance. . . . God will never give up on you.

I pray God will bless your friendships. . . . I know how much you desire a deep friendship with someone who "gets" you. Understands what you're feeling. Someone who takes seriously when you are wounded emotionally. And someone who believes in your dreams. I'm praying God will bring such a person in your life. A friend who can act silly and be serious. A friend who will keep a confidence and be absolutely trustworthy.

I am praying God will grow our hearts together as mom and daughter. . . . I love you forever, there's no one like you, and I wouldn't change being your mom for anything. You make me smile. You cause me to pray! (Smile) I love you, sweet girl, and if you ever doubt it, well, reread this note.

And so I did—pray. There were times Kristen didn't particularly like it. There were lots of times I didn't particularly want to. But hey, One Tough Mother sucks it up and just does it anyway, right?

And so God answered—in the most incrementally small ways ever known to motherkind! (Patience isn't one of my greatest strengths. So sue me.)

There's no hocus-pocus theology at work here, mind you. It was simply God showing up and proving himself faithful in the life of this One Tough Mother and, hey, let me be honest here, her One Tough Mother Mini-me offspring!

Kristen's still hashing through her faith, and that's more than okay. But the callousness has lifted, and she'd tell you today without a shadow of a doubt that God and her mom never gave up on her . . . ever.

The first day of her freshman year of college, Kristen met Nicky Durham. They "clicked" and I couldn't help but cry when she told me over the phone a couple of months later, "Mom, Nicky is the friend you have been praying for me to find the last four years." Man, oh, man, you can't beat

## Simple and Sweet: Prayers for Children

"Dear God, thank you for my family, my home, and my pets. Some kids don't have these things. Help me know how I can share with someone. And help me know how to show them you love them. Amen."

"God, thank you for listening to me right now. I'm scared for my friend _____. He's moving, and he's scared and doesn't want to go. Help him find new friends and be happy again. Let him know you are there. Amen."

"God, I'm really, really mad at my sister right now! She just broke my favorite _____. Show me what to do. Amen."

"God, today I made a mistake. I did something I shouldn't have. Please forgive me and help me not to do that again. Amen."[2]

that. Or can you? Because get this—it turns out Nicky is the daughter of my first ever landlords, Wendell and Telesa Durham, and I actually saw Nicky when she was only a few weeks old way back in 1987. (What are the chances? It's as if there were some divine being gloriously intersecting his plans with ours.) Go figure. And Kristen and I have grown stronger together as mother and daughter. As mother and friend.

So how about you? What specific needs do you need to start praying about for your son or daughter?

Let me encourage you to do it—no matter how impossible the need may be. No matter how far gone you think the situation may have become. No matter how little faith you may have to pray. Just do it—and pray honestly. After all,

God already knows what you're thinking and what you're going to say before you ever do, so just say it.

Just pray it.

Find a notebook or perhaps write in some of the wide white margins of your own Bible and note when you prayed (month/day/year), what you prayed, and then when it was answered. This is a must for One Tough Mothers because we just too easily forget. I can't stand up and walk two feet without forgetting why I stood up in the first place. So write it down—and follow through with the "say it out loud" edict of this chapter. Tell your son you're praying he does well in football practice. Tell your daughter you're praying she can better comprehend her sixth-grade math class. Tell them and love them and leave nothing unspoken (or un-prayed).

# My Kingdom for a Slingshot

## Nonnegotiable #9: Face Your Giants

*Would you rather . . .*
supervise twelve potty-training toddlers for twelve hours in a twelve-by-twelve room by yourself
*or*
look your parents in the eye and tell them you're not going to discipline their grandchild the way they think it should be done?
*Would you rather . . .*
publish your journal/diary for public consumption
*or*
stand before your local school board (made up of men and women you interact with every day) and voice your outrage regarding what you believe to be a teacher's inexcusably boorish behavior?
*Would you rather . . .*
hit every red light for the rest of your life

*or*

audibly question a pediatric pulmonary specialist's diagnosis of your child's health problems and tell him you are getting a second opinion?

*Would you rather . . .*

skip this chapter

*or*

stand against your giants?

Right about now I wish so much that I could step through the pages of this book, wrap my arms around you, give you a big obnoxious Julie hug, and visit with you over a cup of hot cocoa and a dozen glazed Krispy Kreme doughnuts while you tell me your story.

Your story of growing up and the relationship you had or have with your mother.

Your story of the kind of mom you thought you'd be or perhaps never be if you could help it.

Your story of conception (sans certain details, of course), including perhaps the unexpected nature of a pregnancy or the aching longing and waiting over months and years for a safe, full-term delivery.

As I bite into doughnut number three, I'd listen to your story of adoption and squeeze your hand as you describe the dizzy and tumultuous emotional, spiritual, and financial ride involved in the long and arduous process.

I'd listen to your stories of victories and defeats.

I'd listen to your stories of dreams and disappointments.

And if you counted me trustworthy, I'd listen as you named the taunting and intimidating giants robbing you of One Tough Mother rest emotionally, physically, mentally, and spiritually. Then, when at last we found ourselves talked out, I would take your hands, look you straight in the eyes, and tell you, "I'm going to stay right here with you as you stand against (and defeat) every giant you named."

See, I never said being One Tough Mother was going to be easy; nothing of substantive value ever is. But I did mention way, way back in chapter 3 that we were never meant to go it alone. And I meant it. For the remaining pages in this chapter I want you to picture me right there with you— facing those grandparents, talking to those school board members, questioning that well-educated physician, and tagging along as you confront, defeat, and silence anything or anyone standing between you and One Tough Mother peace.

## Who or What Are Giants?

Beth Moore, in her book *Praying God's Word*, speaks of strongholds and their insidious power to cripple our lives. As I read her definition, I realized replacing the word *stronghold* with the word *giant* could aptly define the problem we face with giants.

> A [giant] is anything that exalts itself in our minds, "pretending" to be bigger or more powerful than our God. [A giant] steals much of our focus and causes us to feel overpowered. Controlled. Mastered. Whether [the giant] is an addiction, unforgiveness towards a person who has hurt us, or despair over a loss, it is something that consumes so much of our emotional and mental energy that abundant life is strangled—our callings remain largely unfulfilled and our believing lives are virtually ineffective.[1]

Man, oh, man, does that definition ever strike home.
A giant saps our strength.
A giant calls the shots.
A giant taunts us and reminds us of our past failures.
A giants mocks our attempts to move forward.

A giant has a seemingly unstoppable or unbeatable strength.

A giant oftentimes seems bigger than God himself.

The fear of a giant coupled with hesitancy to stand against it will, without question, render your mothering life all but ineffective.

There are as many types of giants as there are women reading this book, but I'd like to list a few that seem to be common to motherkind. Feel free to scribble in the name of yours if it has been overlooked. Now realize, please, when I list certain types of people in the following list, I am not saying they are evil or bad. The last thing I want is for you pick up five smooth stones and start hurling them at Grandma!

I don't believe *every* giant we need to stand against as One Tough Mother is necessarily spiritual in nature. I mention specific types of people because I have found mothers often have a difficult time standing up to people who, sometimes based on sheer status, position, or relational intimacy, come to represent a giant in their minds. I'm *not* telling you to throw a Bible at them, scream "Repent!" and then hightail it the other way. I am suggesting, however, that it will be necessary for some of you reading these pages to plant your feet, establish some new boundaries, and stand up to those you have cowered to despite knowing you should do otherwise. Some of our giants need to discover we do indeed have a backbone, and we're not afraid to use it!

I've also included emotional giants which so easily cripple a mother's heart and convince it to quit. And I would submit that these are indeed spiritual in nature and require a spiritual tactic to successfully confront and conquer.

### Giant #1: Our Parents

It can be the best of times.
It can be the worst of times.

You're trying to figure out who you are as a new mom—discovering your way of doing things with your baby (then figuring it out with a toddler, a preschooler, a junior high kid, and a teenager) and all the while listening to the thoughts, opinions, and still very, very parental voice of your mother and father—even your grandparents, perhaps.

I distinctly recall the afternoon we brought Kristen home from the hospital to our first apartment in Hannibal, Missouri. My parents and grandmother were awaiting our arrival and quickly huddled around me as I carried Kristen into the living room.

"She should have warmer clothes on," my mother stated.

(It was the hottest summer on record at that time.)

"And her little skin still looks yellow—I'd be worried sick!" she added for effect.

(We had already discussed Kristen's jaundice with our pediatrician, and Kristen would be sunning herself from her bassinet a few minutes every day once we arrived home.)

"She's been sleeping an awfully long time," my dad then observed. "Maybe you need to wake her up."

(After ten minutes of attempting to awaken Sleeping Beauty, I gave up.)

"She's probably not getting enough milk, and that's why she's sleeping so much," my grandma then noted.

(Uh, thanks, Grandma—like I wasn't worried about that already!)

Remember those days? Or maybe you're living them now—nursing a three-week-old and just starting to experience what you've read in the paragraphs above. Or perhaps you've recently been thrown into the world of mothering with nary a warning: the phone call came through, the adoption details were all settled, and suddenly here you are—a new mom trying to figure out all the details.

No one looms larger than life more than one's parents. What they think.

What they imply.

What they say.

And how they believe we should go about things—especially when it comes to *their* grandchildren.

### Giant #2: Doctors

Have you ever spent a morning waiting with a sick child to see your family doctor, then been called back to wait some more in an examining room, then heard a knock on the door and watched as the doctor entered the room, stayed a few minutes, stood up, shook your hand, and told you to wait for the nurse to write out the prescription your child was going to need—then watched him leave the room only to ask yourself, "What the heck was that?"

Maybe it was the white lab coat she was wearing or the stethoscope dangling around her neck. Perhaps it was seeing the wall display highlighting her educational degrees and realizing they represented the same amount of years you'd spent laying out working on a great tan. Whatever "it" may be the cause, I know I'm not the only one who has been struck mute when meeting a doctor or when thinking about standing up to them as a mom.

I recall one incident in particular. My two oldest children returned home from elementary-aged church camp with a few more things than they had left home with. Ugh. You know where this story's going, don't you?

Siblings.

Summer camp.

Shared brushes.

Head lice.

It was my first encounter with those nasty little nits, and at the time my daughter had ringlet curls spiraling down past her shoulder blades—oh, and school was scheduled to begin in less than one week. I was at a loss as to what I should do.

One friend suggested the old time "cure" of soaking her hair and scalp in kerosene. ("Are you completely nuts?" I asked her.)

Another told me to slather mayonnaise on her scalp, cover it with plastic wrap, and let it sit for ten hours to suffocate the intruders. (*Um, after ten hours won't her head be spoiled?* I wondered.)

I spoke with the few women I wasn't too embarrassed to call—after all, we're supposed to control the lice thing, aren't we?—and finally decided to make an appointment with our doctor and deal with it according to his medical opinion.

Once he confirmed the problem was indeed head lice, he prescribed a super-powerful shampoo potion containing the pesticide—pesticide!—lindane.

And I thought my kerosene friend was crazy.

I wasn't sure about this at all but drove to the pharmacy and picked up the prescription shampoo anyway. I drove home and followed the directions carefully, applying it to my kids' dry hair and thoroughly rubbing it into the hair and scalp. I left it on for four minutes, worked it into a lather with a small amount of water, and then rinsed it out thoroughly as each child bent their head over our deep, white porcelain kitchen sink

I repeated said hair washings one week later, all the while fighting back an unrelenting "this just doesn't seem right" hincky mom feeling.

I didn't call the doctor to question his orders.

I didn't obey my mom feelings.

I kept silent and just told myself I was worrying over nothing.

About four months later we signed up for dial-up Internet service and I found myself scouring the Internet. Listen, I

164 · One Tough Mother

am a reference and information junkie. You may recall my mentioning how much I enjoyed reading the encyclopedias at Murle Woolston's house as a little girl. Well, having access to the World Wide Web was a million times better than a set of hardbound tomes. I could type in keywords and find details about anything and everything. So one day I typed in the words *lindane* and *lice* at www.about.com and read something similar to this:

"Beware of lindane! Be aware that the Food and Drug Administration has issued warnings as to the safe use of this very powerful pesticide. For kids who are smaller, more medically fragile, or more neurologically impaired, it may not be worth the risk."[2]

I thought I was going to throw up on my keyboard. I anxiously typed and clicked my way to www.webmd.com, only to find similar warnings reading much like the information posted there today:

> Lindane may be used when other products fail to get rid of lice or when a person cannot use any of the other products. The shampoo may be used to treat head lice. Lindane was the drug of choice for treating lice for many years. However, permethrin (Nix) is currently the preferred treatment because it is more effective and is less likely to cause side effects. When used as directed, lindane is safe and has few side effects. However, it is easily absorbed into the skin and can cause negative side effects when it is not used properly. If lindane is left on the skin too long, used repeatedly, or eaten, it can cause nervous system side effects, such as seizures, especially in young children.[3]

I knew something wasn't right!

I must have kicked myself a hundred times that day as I asked myself over and over why I didn't push my doctor when first concerned about the prescription. I easily spent four hours jumping from website to website in an attempt to calm my nerves and convince myself I hadn't irreparably harmed my son and daughter.

I promised myself then and there that I would never again stifle my motherly concerns and misgivings with a physician of any kind. Unbeknownst to me at the time, I established the One Tough Mother nonnegotiable of facing my giant.

### Giant #3: School Administration/Teachers

It was Ricky's fifth grade year and we were on our way to find out whose class he had been placed in.

I was a nervous wreck.

See, there was one teacher in particular whom Ricky did not want to get, and it was the one teacher in particular whom I did not want to get Ricky.

I'm a realist when it comes to interpersonal relations, and I knew my son and this fifth-grade teacher well enough to recognize the sheer folly of placing them in the same classroom. You know what I'm talking about, moms.

Some of our little guys are quiet and thrive in a teacher-led environment of calm, quiet, and gentleness. Some of our sons are rambunctious and need a high-energy teacher who appreciates the "boyishness" of being a boy and doesn't back down to their raucous way of expressing themselves. And some of our sons are simply a bad match from the get-go with certain teacher personalities.

So as we walked through the doors and approached the bulletin board splayed with class lists, I simply held my breath and anxiously read each fifth-grade heading.

I think it was Ricky Neal's plaintive wail that first alerted me to the not-so-good news. Glancing quickly to my left, I read the teacher's name and saw my son's listed beneath.

Not good.

Now, I don't want you to think I was some kind of "You'd better do what I say because this is my little baby and he never does anything wrong and I want to tell you how to do everything" type mom. On the contrary, I rarely made comments about such things and had never filed a complaint of any sort with the principal—or other teachers, for that matter. I have a teaching degree myself and appreciate the work it takes to corral and educate a roomful of squirrelly kids. But the prospect of this teacher and my son being in the same room together for nearly nine months, well, it was just unacceptable in my book.

So I decided to speak with the principal and request a room change.

*Sigh.*

Here's the crazy thing about it: I was nearly thirty-five years old. I had been a substitute teacher for the school numerous times. And I knew the principal well enough. But as soon as I entered his office, my stomach churned, my knees grew weak, and I felt about what an actual fifth-grader would feel when facing the principal.

Good grief!

You'd have thought I'd just learned to speak, the way I hemmed and hawed and stammered. It probably took me fifteen minutes just to get to the point of my visit. But get there I did—eventually—and I laid out my case for Ricky's transfer to another teacher's classroom.

The principal said he couldn't promise me anything and let me know he wasn't all that pleased with my even asking. I reiterated my reasons for doing so and just wanted to get out of his office as quickly as possible. Two days later I received a letter saying Ricky Neal had been moved to another class and that as of the date of the letter, no further considerations would be made or acted upon regarding future parental requests such as mine.

Whew.

That was one of the first administrative giants I ever faced, and I lived to tell the tale despite my insecurity. Looking back, I am so thankful I did it. Facing the giant of classroom procedure, protocol, and administrative leadership shored up my One Tough Mother reserves and prepared me for far greater battles ahead.

## Giant #4: Another Mom

One of the most formidable giants you will ever face may wear heels, stand less than five feet six inches tall, carry a purse, and sit beside you during your daughter's volleyball games.

In all likelihood she tells you what she thinks she's doing right and implies you're doing something wrong. She may be what I refer to as a "basement person"—someone who somehow manages to bring you down when it comes to life and motherhood in general. Basement moms have a knack for bringing your children's deficiencies and weaknesses to the forefront, and often after leaving their company you may find yourself looking at your kids and questioning why you ever thought you could do this job of parenting.

I lived in a community with one such petite giant many, many years ago. No matter what my kids did— one child especially—she always seemed to find a way to criticize or belittle their efforts during conversation between us. She would point out a certain behavior, shake her head, lower her voice, and say, "I really don't know how you put up with that child." And sometimes it was as much what she didn't say as what she did. There's nothing like a chasm of silence to scream out a giant's influence.

Looking back as a forty-one-year-old mother, I can't imagine why I put up with her garbage as long as I did. I was a pretty confident mother during those first ten years of raising my three kids, and I had never been a shrinking violet when it came to voicing my own opinion. But for some reason, another mother intimidated me.

Maybe you've know a few women like that too. (Who knows? Maybe some of us reading these pages are that mother!) If so, be assured you are not the only mom who ever needed to face the mommy giant.

## Giant #5: Fear

As I mentioned in the beginning pages of this chapter, I firmly believe some of the giants we face as moms are spiritual in nature. Something more is going on than merely what our eyes and ears and senses can discern. Giant strongholds are crippling mothers' ability to think straight and embrace truth, and the giant of fear looms over us nearly twelve feet tall.

Remember, a giant is something that consumes so much of our emotional and mental energy that abundant life is strangled—our callings remain largely unfulfilled and our believing lives are virtually ineffective. Does any giant in your life have the power to create such a debilitating list of "Things I'm Afraid Of" as writer and journalist Lindsey O'Connor compiled?

> *Invisible Things:* Carbon monoxide. Radon. Carpet, paint, and furniture emissions. Ozone. U.V. rays. Lead in the dirt. Who knows what in the water. Asbestos.
>
> 102.5 degree fever.
>
> *Formerly Useful Now Lethal Things:* Games with tiny parts. Hard candies. Deflated balloons. Plastic bags.

Hazardous chemicals that actually clean your house. Glass. Hot dogs that are not split lengthwise.

103.2 degree fever.

*Ingested Things:* salmonella, preservatives, red dye, mercury, E-coli. Pennies.

*The Other Hand Things:* Germs require antibacterial soap; on the other hand C9 super viruses. Preschoolers require apple juice, apple sauce, and apples; on the other hand C9 pesticides. Automatically immunizing requires rethinking; on the other hand, measles, mumps, rubella.

Toxic mold. Flesh-eating bacteria. 103.9 degree fever.

*The What-If Things:* What if he rides his Power Wheels into a car? What if she picks up biting at play group? What if Winnie-the-Pooh suffocates her in the night?

*Nature Things:* Fire ants. Wasps. Hornets. Copperheads. Baby garter snakes (because you never can be too sure).

*Sharp Things:* Sticks. Hangers. Forks. Scissors. Because, all together now, "You'll poke your eye out!"

105 degree fever.

*Unspeakable Things:* Unconsciousness. Abductions.

*Unthinkable Things:* That I'll not be enough. That I'll not be there.

And this is my child's "Things I am Afraid Of" list: *Nothing.*

Which exponentially adds to my fear list.[4]

The giant of fear whispers, "You can't do this because you're too scared."

The giant of fear will cost you more than you want to pay in your relationships and your mothering.

The giant of fear will leave you miserable and stunted.

The giant of fear will mock your thoughts even now as you begin to shore up your confidence and allow yourself to believe you can face this giant and annihilate it once and for all.

Ladies, may I suggest you tell the giant of fear to shut up and go away!

## Slingshot Strategies

So here we are, One Tough Mothers desiring to get on with our lives and past the giant(s) standing in our way. It's high time we picked up our slingshot and a few smooth stones and put them to good use. So here they are: seven strategic stones to use at your discretion and for your benefit. Each one is powerful enough to fell more than one Goliath.

### Accept that giants will always be in your life.

Forget about thinking you can get to someplace where no more giant issues will arise. (You sooooooooooo need to forget that.) You were hoping otherwise, perhaps? Sorry. But this isn't such bad news, really. You can sigh with relief knowing that all of us will periodically have someone or something in our lives as moms (and as women, but that's another book) which obnoxiously proclaims itself unde-featable. The good news about that not-so-great reality is that you can prepare yourself. You don't have to be caught off guard or find yourself one stone short of a giant-felling load. Nope.

Those giants will come and you, my dear One Tough Mother, can and will be prepared to contend with them in a forthright and successful manner.

Facing this truth is where you want to start because even if you somehow managed to dispel all the "giant" people in your life; even if you knocked down and out all the "giant" circumstances of your past, present, and future; even if you learned how to tame the "giant" of your fears, or worries, or whatever, you would still face more. Why is that? Well, here's what I have found to be true: all of us, no matter where we live geographically on this fabulous planet called Earth, will contend at some time with a culture setting itself against many of the things we desire as One Tough Mother.

I'm typing the final portion of this chapter in Eastern Europe. I have spent two weeks speaking to mothers in Vienna, Austria; at a military base in Wiesbaden, Germany; and in the cities of Debrecen and Budapest, Hungary.

Debrecen sits approximately three hours outside the capital and, like Budapest, was until eighteen years ago governed by the Communist Party.

Then in 1989, everything changed—out went the old (well, sorta; some of the old simply changed their party name, put on a new suit, and signed up for another political go-around) and in came freedom and independence.

Perhaps it is not possible for those who have grown up with freedom to comprehend the oppressive weight of such a culture. I know I certainly cannot. I can, however, listen to the stories of those who did. And time and time again, I was struck by how similar many of our stories were.

Why is that? How can a mother raising a child in Communist Hungary have the same story as one going through the motions in western Illinois? How is it that we battle so many of the same giants? I believe it is in no small part due to the fact that we all live in a broken world, a broken culture—be it Hungarian or American. As I said, we can attempt to rid ourselves of various giants, but we will always have to contend for, with, and against the culture in which we live.

172 · One Tough Mother

Chances are good (very good, in fact) that we all will find ourselves swimming upstream in the culture around us, be it as the One Tough Mother of babies, toddlers, preteens, or teenagers. None of us will ever live on a continent or in a country, province, city, or village in which everyone agrees (or even wants) to support the nonnegotiables we choose to adhere to as moms. None of us. As a result, there will always be people and thought systems and, yes, even governments that oppose us. But if we continue to grasp and live out these nonnegotiables—and I do mean truly grasp and own them for ourselves—well, I believe fewer of us will be conformed to the culture around us.

### Offer a tempered response to your giants.

Opposition doesn't have to be ugly or all-or-nothing (but if it comes to that, One Tough Mother is comfortable with it). The last thing I'd want you to do after reading this chapter is to think you can (or should) go thwack your giants on the forehead verbally or physically. Goodness! That would put us into an entirely different tough mom category.

No, the second strategy stone I want you to pick up is that of well-thought-out and seasoned actions and responses to the giant currently before you. There's no excuse for anything else when it comes to this area. For one thing, impulsive overreacting doesn't do us any good in the long run, and for another, well, it doesn't do us any good. Period.

Maybe you're different than me, but part of my all-or-nothing One Tough Mother temperament always seemed to take me to the highest of highs and lowest of lows. In those early years of trying to figure out how to confront my giants, I seemed to either back off altogether (hmm, I wasn't exactly facing them, was I?) or find myself tied up in emotional and mental knots. And sometimes, yes, sometimes I spoke words and thoughts that I'd just as soon forget—as would those who heard them.

Sigh. But you know what they say: all is not lost. Those not-so-great memories have taught me a few things, and this is one of utmost importance: it is possible to oppose the voices, opinions, culture, and such without making an absolute mess of our relationships and situations. It doesn't always have to be all-or-nothing. In fact, I'd go as far as to say it rarely has to go that far. If you find yourself engaging a parent, in-law, or other relative, you don't have to allow the situation to escalate to a point where irreparable harm is done. You don't have to cut grandparents out completely, in most cases. (As always, this rule has exceptions, and I encourage you to seek out wise counsel if you feel matters have progressed to such a stage.) If an authority figure such as a doctor or administrative leader in your child's educational system is casting a long and foreboding shadow, do by all means stand up for your child and yourself. Let your concerns be heard—clearly and strongly. Just do so without engaging in cursing, gossip, or childish behavior yourself.

### *Love keeps us balanced.*

Remember that timeless line from *The Princess Bride* as Buttercup and Prince Humperdinck are about to be joined in holy matrimony? "Wuv, twuw wuv." Ah, that's what it's all about when it comes to keeping your perspective when staring down a giant. Love, true love, helps us see the problem instead of the person. Love helps us—equips and enables us—to not take things personally and to keep our cool. Without love I'd be slappin' up the heads of a lot of people and probably living a life of fear and worry and dismay. Not exactly the ideal One Tough Mother.

*Let your giants inspire you to go deeper.*

Okay, I have it on good authority from one of the friends named on the dedication page that resistance training makes you stronger. It seems all those ladies standing in a room at the local YMCA pulling on rubber bands the size of my waistband are actually accomplishing something! Becky said something about muscles growing, but I was finishing up my snack of peanut M&M's and couldn't exactly hear her well over the crunching.

Nevertheless, I'll take her word for it.

All that to say this (and "this" I actually know a thing or two about due to personal experience and living for forty-one years): you and I have a monumental choice to make when deciding to take on those giants. We can allow them to either destroy us as moms or inspire us as One Tough Mother.

When I (and my husband and daughter) had to deal with problems at Kristen's school a couple of years ago, we all came to the same conclusion: I can do this, I'm going to do this, and I'm going to allow all of what happens to make me stronger.

I have a favorite part in the Bible which encourages everyone to be "rooted, established, and built up" in their faith (see Colossians 2:7 NASB). This is exactly what I want for you! I want you—as a result of facing the giants with integrity, grace, and determination—to be a mother who is rooted, established, and built up in her ability to stand and do what is right.

I want you to be a mother who is rooted, established, and built up in going deeper with the nonnegotiables she has come to own. And to be inspired by the rich, rewarding, "you can't touch this!" sense of pride that comes as a result. Giants do not have to destroy you! In fact, you can come to a place of thanksgiving (which, funny enough, is mentioned in the second portion of that favorite verse) for the very giants you have met. The giant really isn't all that powerful, not really; the giant has power only to the degree we lend and afford it.

My children's doctor (mentioned earlier in this chapter) wasn't the enemy. He wasn't bad. He wasn't mean. He was just the children's doctor. But as a result of my experience with him, I was inspired to learn more about my children's health in order to be knowledgeable and "rooted, established, and built up" in my own role as their mother. I was inspired to take a more hands-on approach to all things medical, and as a result, when Patrick was born and dealt with apnea and asthma for the first five years of his life, I was One Tough Mother who spoke up and sought out (uh, demanded) the treatment I felt he needed and that was available. I wasn't overly obnoxious. I simply stood my ground and looked more than one medical specialist in the face and asked one more question.

### *Acknowledge those who AREN'T giants.*

No surprise here: we can get so caught up in pinpointing our giants that we fail to appreciate and number those who are *for* us! We can forget those who are by our side and who sometimes hold us up when we grow weary in the mothering race. We have another choice to make as One Tough Mother at this particular juncture. We can decide to become either better or bitter—and appreciating those who are on our team is one sure way to be better rather than bitter.

One close friend shared with me how the death of her twenty-two-hour-old son and the fear of what could lie ahead genetically in future children and pregnancies could have easily become an insurmountable giant of bitterness and fear. Yet the love and support of her parents, her husband, her inner circle group of friends, and her relentless, pursuing God enabled her to choose to become better. And they ultimately equipped her to reach for the final giant-felling stone we'll get to in just a bit.

### Take your giants down to size.

Okay, homework assignment for you. Go outside around 10:00 a.m. or 2:00 p.m. on a sunny day and find a sidewalk, driveway, or safe side street. Take a look at your shadow! Remember childhood days when you and a best friend would walk along and laugh at the gargantuan silhouette you projected with the sun behind you. Now consider the giant you face and realize this: your attitude and perspective is like the sun beaming upon the giant. It can lengthen its reach and widen its power. Or, as is the case around noon, it can significantly decrease it.

So which will it be?

Consider this true story: One of the giants staring bug-eyed at a woman traveling Europe with me for two weeks was the fear of bridges. Not so much the bridge itself . . . well, okay, it was the bridge itself, but this giant brought along its first cousin: fear of a vehicle losing control while driving on the bridge and plummeting over the side.

Scary giant indeed.

Now, here's the thing. This fear could have kept my friend from taking this once-in-a-lifetime trip to three of the most beautiful countries in the world. But a few non-giant friends encouraged her to go and deal with things as they came. So she did. And so we found ourselves in a white minivan tooling across the Chain Bridge in Budapest, Hungary, with my friend riding smack-dab in the middle seat, front row.

Rut, roh! I didn't know what my friend was going to do. None of us who knew about her giant did. So we just said a quiet prayer and watched.

She never flinched.

She never cried.

She never threw herself on the dashboard and huddled up into a tight ball.

Nope. My friend just turned her head from side to side and took in all the magnificent sights of a city with history going back as far as 896. A few hours later when we were all congratulating her on keeping her cool, she replied, "Oh, I never really thought too much about it. There was just too much to see not to look, and I wasn't about to waste my time with my eyes closed."

Attitude.

Perspective.

They are a lethal combination when it comes time to knock a few giants over.

### *Help others fight their giants.*

This final stone is the one my friend chose to pick up after she became better rather than bitter. Helping others name, face, and deal with their giants out of our own experience, success, and sorrow is perhaps the most fulfilling of our slingshot strategies.

Who better than the woman who knows the devastating loss of losing a child to speak to the woman paralyzed by her own sorrow after the death of a child? Who better than the woman who knows what it is like to contend with worry and fear for her future and those of any children yet to be born?

Who better than the woman who has stared down an intangible giant of fear (such as crossing bridges) to speak to the woman paralyzed by her own worry over the unknown and unpredictable?

See, when we choose to help others, we step outside ourselves. We choose to live bigger than our own life and experience. We free women from the impossibly insane notion that they are the only ones who have succumbed to such fear, worry, frustration, and doubt.

And here's the great thing: you don't have to be completely through all your stuff to speak to others. You can speak while you still struggle. But mind you, if the giant's saber is still in your side—it's too soon. I've listened to a few women speak before it was time. It was painful to watch and painful to see. Rather than speaking of healing, they were a wound speaking. So give yourself time. You don't have to prove some freaky One Tough Mother toughness. Speak out of your healing rather than your woundedness.

Giants steal the peace God gives us as mothers.

Giants keep us from the purposes God has planned for us as mothers.

Giants rob us of the good things God has given us for our success and job; they freeze our faith, our thinking, our actions, and will ultimately destroy us if we don't straighten our backbone, plant our feet, and set our gaze squarely ahead toward our change and their defeat.

It is possible for us to face the giants standing before us and those hiding in the shadows.

It is possible to become One Tough Mother.

# 12

# You're Only a Failure If You Quit, Like, Forever

## Nonnegotiable #10: Never Give Up

Here's a shocker for you—agree or disagree as you like: one common error we all make, one that has serious consequences as we step out to be One Tough Mother, is the belief that failure is the opposite of success. Intellectually we know better, but emotionally we often fail to act on what we know to be true when it comes to ourselves.

Think about the many times you have introduced your child to a new activity, like putting on a sock (oh, the horrors that memory brings to mind!), drawing a circle, tying a shoelace, hitting a ball with a bat, or working out a mathematical equation for school. Quite often the child failed to accomplish the activity the first time and perhaps became frustrated, angry, and even tearful in response to their lack of success—to their failure.

Now you, being the mom, had innumerable automatic responses you spoke back to them. Phrases such as, "Don't worry, you'll get better with practice," and "Nobody does it right the first time," and "Anything really important takes time and effort."

As the mom and as the adult in the relationship, you clearly realized that failure (real and perceived) is just a step on the road to success. That's why you showed your child again and again how to loop one lace over the other. That's why you bought big boy underpants and big girl panties and walked with them the fourteen steps to the big kid potty time after time after time after time. That's why you stayed with all of it (parenting) and all of them (children)—for you know it is impossible to succeed without first failing.

This concept is one many of us learned as a basic science principle during our eighth-grade year of junior high: an experiment is never truly a failure; it's a lesson. It teaches us what *not* to do and pushes us to look for another approach until we find one that works.

We filled beakers with liquid and set rubbing alcohol aflame on lab counters. (Why are you looking at me like that? Like I was the only delinquent in a junior high school science classroom?) We dissected earthworms and nearly passed out from the wicked vapors of formaldehyde. And most of us passed the class and begrudgingly learned that when it comes to the success of an experiment, to try, try again is the key.

So why then do we find it so hard to apply such knowledge to our mothering?

Why is everything so all-or-nothing in our measurement of being a successful mom? And why does "successful" mothering almost always have to do with the details of how our children turned out—or didn't turn out, as is more often the case—rather than with how open we are to what

God is doing with us in the midst of the frazzled messes and ecstatic joys?

Sometimes I seem to have more questions than answers as a writer. But asking the *right* question is just what we need to do when it comes to getting a healthy view of failure and motherhood. Carla Barnhill, former editor of *Christian Parenting Today* and author of the book *The Myth of the Perfect Mother*, was asked, "Can we measure our success as a mom?" and this was her rather unconventional response:

> Honestly, our focus should be on living faithfully in everything we do: in our parenting, our marriage, our friendships, and our work. And lives of faith always include failure, because we're works in progress. Every parent on the planet makes mistakes, so instead of beating ourselves up for all the ways we aren't perfect, we can seek God in our failures and allow him to redeem them in our lives and in the lives of our children. The only real failure in motherhood is to close ourselves off to what God's doing in our lives, to focus so intently on our children that we miss the opportunities for growth and formation God has set all around us.[1]

Sometimes it seems the only opportunity for growth and formation I've managed to seize in the last twenty years is an ever more alarming increase in the perimeter of my upper thighs. But I'm pretty sure Carla Barnhill was referring to something completely different in her writing—quite sure, in fact.

As I read "The only real failure in motherhood is to close ourselves off to what God's doing in our lives, to focus so intently on our children that we miss the opportunities for growth and formation God has set all around us," the word *persistence* keeps coming to my mind.

Persistence reminds me of a delightful scene from *Finding Nemo* when Dory, a forgetful but ever-so-tenacious regal tang fish, zips around with energetic high speed and cheers the flagging faith of Marlin the clown fish. She wisely counsels, "Hey there, Mr. Grumpy Gills. When life gets you down, do you wanna know what you've gotta do? Just keep swimming. Just keep swimming. Just keep swimming, swimming, swimming. What do we do? We swim, swim!"

Sometimes we're all a Ms. Grumpy Gills as we look at our failures. And the last thing we are able to see is an opportunity for growth and formation. If you're like me, everything in you wants to simply sink to the bottom of the fishbowl. But persistence (and wisdom) cries out, "Just keep swimming. Just keep swimming. Swimming, swimming, swimming."

I think Carla Barnhill is onto something as she challenges us to take our eyes off of the myth of perfect mothering (as well as its twin myth of raising perfect children) and to look instead for the myriad opportunities God invites us to join him to help us develop personal growth and spiritual formation in the midst of being One Tough Mother.

I wrote the following letter* back in the dark ages (pre-email and IM, in 1999) to a friend of mine when she hit a particularly disheartening spot as a mom, and I am struck by my own Dory challenge to just keep swimming and remain persistent.

*A true writer keeps copies of everything they write! Who knows when it will be fodder for inspiration or chapter content? And just for the record, my friend gave her permission to share my note with you. One Tough Mother always confirms such matters before going to print.

Never forget, Diana, the lives of all moms always, always, always include tales of failure. And I'm talking BIG-time failure. All of us were, are, and forever will be imperfect and fallible. Heaven knows you do not (and should not) have all of life and motherhood figured out at this point in your life.

Sarah is only four years old, and newborn Aaron has you on your "my boobs hurt" lactating mommy toes around the clock.

Diana, relax and inhale a deep, soothing breath, my sweet friend—and don't forget to exhale. Relax and consciously choose to stay with it—right where you are today and right where you'll be tomorrow and a week from tomorrow and even a month from tomorrow—wiping dirty bottoms, reading Mercer Mayer books, and doling out kisses and fruit snacks.

Rest, relax, and know the fate of your children does not rest squarely upon your weary, disillusioned, and imperfect shoulders but with the One whose shoulders are broad, whose heart is mercy, and whose love for you and those babies goes beyond anything you can imagine.

Franklin D. Roosevelt once said, "The only thing we have to fear is fear itself." And nothing could be truer. Fear yields its greatest manipulative control when it is unspoken, unacknowledged, and unrecognized. Once fear—great and small—is exposed, it quickly and consistently loses its ability to hold us hostage. And I can't help but wonder (and believe) that fear is one of the chief components in our compulsion to overthink so many parenting factors.

We fear we won't do something right.

We fear we'll do something wrong.

We fear we can't and won't do *everything* right.

We fear we will make decisions and they will be the wrong decisions.

We fear we will do our best and our best, well, our best just won't cut it.

We fear *failure*.

But any of us reading these pages knows failure is part and parcel of being a mom.

We will coach our child's T-ball team and stand helplessly by as the future Hall of Famer for whom we purchased a bat, ball helmet, and batting gloves dumps a baseball cap full of dirt on two of the children sitting on second base and then gleefully shoves dirt up his nose. (Nice, real nice.)

We will fail to conceive.

We will fail to give birth vaginally.

We will fail to adopt as quickly as our heart and womb scream for a child.

We will shoot for the stars and settle for a low-lying prairie plain.

We will fail.

Yet we will still be Mom.

Accepting failure and not shirking from it helps define us and shape us into One Tough Mother who has learned what is important, what's not, and how to live in the in-between-ness of it all.

Then and only then will we learn to laugh again and to embrace the wildness of this thing called mothering. To revel in the never-ending refreshment of sloppy kisses and knock-knock jokes. And to bask in what must be the closest thing to audible divinity—the roiling sound of giggles emanating from those created for us—our children.

Gosh, it almost makes you want to put down this book and go have another baby!

Encouragement and authenticity is like that. It makes you feel more real and more alive and helps you believe deeper and higher than you could have ever believed without it. Time and time again I cheer from *this* side of the keyboard for my readers and utter rousing cheers of support for audience compatriots with this question: "What good are we as women—as mothers, as daughters, as friends, as authors and readers and believers—if we are not real?"

Hear this, moms: you're only a failure if you quit—like, forever and ever and ever. And I'd be so bold as to say that 99.9 percent of you reading these pages will never, ever do such a thing. But here's the crazy thing. Even if you did (or do) land in that 0.01 percent category, anyone and everyone can find a second chance to restore such failure. It's called grace. And grace longs to restore what we have written off as failure.

God's persistent desire toward us and his faithful commitment to grow us and form us as moms—as women—always, always, always takes place in and through the situations and circumstances in which we currently live. As long as we are living and breathing, we're going to make mistakes and know failure, but a One Tough Mother of persistent character will carefully consider the lessons such failure teaches and will consistently apply such truth to every facet of her life.

Here are a few truths I've learned over the past twenty years. Perhaps one or two will help you accept failure better and enable you to hang tough as One Tough Mother who understands the life-changing lessons to be learned as a result of them.

## We Learn What Works—and What Doesn't—from Failure

Think about the first time you tried to quiet a wailing, inconsolable infant. Maybe it was a sturdy nine-pound baby boy who threatened to raise the roof or the ferocious cries of a deceptively feather-light preemie girl who made your heart melt each time you picked her up. Nevertheless, that baby needed to be "fixed" or to have something "fixed" in order to soothe their screams. So you placed him against your left shoulder, patted his back, and cooed, "There, there," and well, whaddya know, the kid was quiet.

No?

Well, then perhaps you rubbed his belly and that solved the problem?

Still no, huh?

Maybe you laid him across your knees and gently bounced him to dispel any pent-up gas in his tummy? That always works, right?

Oh, then I guess you may have tried to walk around with him for forty-five minutes or so or placed three drops of baby gas drops in his formula and plied him with its sure-to-be-soothing comfort?

The list could go on and on, but eventually you found what worked. *Eventually* that little one was able to relax and stop screaming, and it was the result of your learning from what didn't work and persistently adjusting your mode of mothering until you finally hit on it.

No amount of free advice via the Internet was able to solve your dilemma. No amount of "This always worked for me" offered by your mother, grandmother, or best friend did the trick.

It was your attempts at trying—again and again—and adjusting with each failed venture that eventually led you to the land of peace and quiet. Oftentimes failure alone will bring us to a place where we will listen to new ideas and attempt new ways of solving old problems.

## We Learn Dependence through Failure

I confess: at the heart of my mothering I often have a huge self-sufficient attitude. Too often I believe a quickly rattled prayer and my own ability to get things done is all that is needed for the long haul of being a mom. But my failure quickly (and painfully) reveals the growing sense of ineptitude and helplessness I am unable to overcome by my strength alone. When failure arrives on the front porch of my mothering, God is able to corner me into conclusions I wasn't willing to look at before. And ironically, this inner tension is what God uses to convince me that he alone is the one who can bring me ultimate success in life.

## Through Failure We Realize Our Desperate Need for Grace

I'm so glad the majority of you who will ever read this book did not know me before I became a mother. Really, I am.

I thought I knew pretty much everything, and I opined about such matters to friends and family. Now, I wasn't particularly mean, but if I had watched you at the local Wal-Mart and saw your toddler wigging out in the parking lot over a bunch of dropped Skittles pieces, I would have thought one or two things: "What are you doing feeding your kid Skittles at age two?" and "I will never allow a child of mine to act that obnoxious in public."

Sigh.

Then there's the rest of the story. . . . Real life intervened, and not only did I feed my children Skittles but I, not the children, behaved in such an obnoxious and out-of-control manner in my early, early years of being a mom that it warranted my writing a book about it in an effort to keep other moms from making the same mistake.

Personal sin and failure taught me the urgency and wisdom of clinging to the grace of God in my life. And one of the best definitions I've ever heard describing such grace was spoken by Lulu Roman, former television star of the 1970s classic country variety show *Hee Haw*: "Grace," she said, "is the empowering presence of God in our lives that enables us to be who he has called us to be so we can do what he has called us to do—right where we are."

> Grace is what every mother needs, because even One Tough Mothers don't get it right every time.
>
> Grace tells us without apology that nothing is beyond the redeeming power of God to rescue and restore.
>
> Grace makes us unashamed as mothers.
>
> Grace enables us to trust Someone other than the latest expert or professional or author.
>
> Grace allows us to expel the collective breath of apprehension we've been holding since we made our first mistake.

It's cyclical in nature: We learn to try and try again, learning from our mistakes and embracing what works. And in those failures we learn we are incapable of doing everything ourselves, no matter how spiritual we may consider ourselves or how emotionally or intellectually gifted we may be. And when that realization comes, many of us embrace our complete dependence on God.

That's when the grace begins! For as we acknowledge our failure, grace shapes our thinking and our heart, and we can and do naturally become more and more authentic with one another in regards to our varying shortcomings. When we accept the lavish gift of grace, we begin to expose what's really going on in our minivans and our living rooms when no one else is around. Grace allows us to rest in our success as a mom but even more so in our failure, for this is where God resides.

And then, oh, then, we are at last able to seize hold of hope.

Hope tells us without apology that nothing is beyond the redeeming power of God to rescue and restore.

Hope draws our eyes toward the things that lie ahead and lays to rest, at last, those that lie behind.

Hope allows us to be unashamed as tender One Tough Mothers.

# Appendix

# Maintaining and
# Accessorizing "The Package"

## Body Basics

Your skin radiates head to toe health and sensuality. It is the largest body organ and is responsible for important jobs such as controlling your temperature and protecting your internal organs from the outside world. Needless to say, taking care of it is both wise and practical.

*First things first: soap.* When it comes to overall cleansing of the body and face, you're best off avoiding deodorant soaps, antibacterial soaps, and shower and bath gels. All three have a strong risk of irritating and drying out the skin. Better choices include glycerin soap (like Neutrogena Original Formula Fragrance-Free Facial Cleansing Bar), hand-milled soap (found at Crabtree & Evelyn stores and online shop), exfoliating soap (Burt's Bees has a nice product with citrus spice), and cleansing bars and body washes (one of my personal favorites is Oil of Olay body wash with shea butter. Mmmm, yummy!).

*Second, moisturizers.* Do not skip this part of your One Tough Mother Get Sexy Back regime. Once you've washed (and perhaps exfoliated) yourself clean, you'll want to apply body oil, lotion, or cream while you're still damp. My shower shelves are filled with a number of items, but one product I come back to time and time again is good old baby oil. Say what you will, but I've found it most effective over the course of (gads!) twenty-five years. Body oils work well and can be purchased in a number of packaging types: capsules, dissolving pellets for the bath, and simple squeeze containers.

# Dermatology

Okay, so a certain percentage of us didn't do any of the following tried-and-true recommended suggestions as a teenager or woman in her twenties or even thirties. Instead we slathered on the baby oil and fried ourselves crispy and tan (or not, as the case may be for the more melanin-challenged amongst us). Nevertheless, it's never too early to start—especially after one has tugged two skin tags from one's neck and can connect twenty-plus "sun spots" across one's shoulders and back. You've read 'em before, but they certainly bear repeating:

- Get a dermatologist.
- Try to avoid the sun between 10:00 a.m. and 4:00 p.m. when the sun's rays are the strongest.
- Apply a broad-spectrum sunscreen with a sun protection factor (SPF) of at least 15.
- Reapply sunscreen every two hours when outdoors, even on cloudy days.

- Wear protective, tightly woven clothing such as a long-sleeved shirt and pants. (Okay, I have NEVER done this. Ever. Just thought I needed to add a little truth in advertising.)
- Wear sunglasses and a four-inch-brimmed hat, even when walking short distances. (Ditto the above: NEVER.)
- Stay in the shade whenever possible.
- Avoid reflective surfaces, which can reflect up to 85 percent of the sun's damaging rays.
- If you notice a change in the size, shape, or appearance of a mole, see a dermatologist. Better still, request an appointment solely for the purpose of your dermatologist "mapping" your skin. Documenting mole size and location is One Tough Mother smart and prudent for what lies ahead as we age.

Some women find themselves battling acne long after puberty. If you find yourself contesting with cystic acne or out-of-control pimples and blackheads, consult your doctor and consider various natural and antibiotic treatments. According to AcneTalks.com,

> Erythromycin, Clindamycin, and sulfa drugs are some of the effective topical medications that can be applied directly to the lesions and so have less possibility of side effects. . . .
> Retinoids are also effective but they may take some time to work. A side effect of retinoids is increased sun sensitivity.
> Benzoyl peroxide is a familiar medication for acne and kills the bacteria that cause acne. Doctors often use benzoyl peroxide along with topical antibiotics to reduce the likelihood of antibiotic resistance. But, benozyl peroxide often causes irritation. . . .
> Tetracyclines are the most frequently prescribed oral antibiotics. Because bacteria tend to develop resistance,

doctors use systemic antibiotics for short-term treatments. Common side effects of tetracyclines are few, but they have been known to cause increased sensitivity to the sun and decreased efficacy of birth control pills in some cases. Minocycline and doxycycline are tetracyclines that can be taken with food and are also less costly.

Another oral treatment is isotretinoin, or retinoic acid (Accutane). Accutane is effective in about two-thirds of the patients who use it to treat more severe cystic acne or acne that is unresponsive to other treatments. Its main side effect is body dryness.[1]

Natural products can be researched thoroughly online. Simply hop onto Google.com and key in phrases such as "healthy natural alternative acne treatment." There are simply too many to list—and I must admit, some of the miracle claims I read are more than a bit suspect. Put on your discernment hat as you surf! For those without online access, I recommend checking out books at your local library, perusing the shelves of your local bookstore, or browsing through the product lines of a department store or local pharmacy store such as Walgreens or CVS. And try contacting your local Avon or Mary Kay consultant for product recommendations—both have proven themselves successful with dermatological products.

# Fragrance

There's a powerful connection between aroma and memory, and taking the time to discover and choose a signature scent helps create and leave an indelible One Tough Mother impression with those we love. Some women will stick with the same fragrance year after year; others will change it up with the varying seasons of life and motherhood. During my pregnancy with Kristen, I wore Giorgio from toe to head. A few years later while mothering Ricky Neal, I went with the more floral scent of Oscar de la Renta. And sure enough, once Patrick arrived I found myself switching fragrances yet again and settled on Chanel No. 5. Now, ten years down the road from my last set of diapers, I've purposely chosen to wear an ultra-sexy fragrance that is altogether about being a woman—Indecence by Givenchy. (It's been discontinued, by the way, so I'm madly buying up creams, lotions, and perfume on eBay.)

# Hair

One Tough Mother can choose a bevy of products to help her create and maintain a healthy, lustrous, and uniquely individual look. Hair salons carry shampoos and conditioners such as Bumble and Bumble, Paul Mitchell, Redken, and Biolage. Less expensive but equally effective (in my opinion) products can be found on the shelves of your local Box-Mart: brands like Kératase, Garnier, and Pantene Pro-V.

For moms fighting dandruff or itching scalp, I've found the over-the-counter Nizoral A-D to be a fabulous alternative to the often stinky and expensive shampoos prescribed by doctors. If you've overdone it with perming, hair coloring, chlorine, or the sun and find your hair damaged, your best option is to cut off as much of the damaged hair as possible and begin a regime of conditioning and restoration. Condition each and every time you wash your hair; detangle hair with a wide-toothed comb; and should you blow-dry or use other heating implements, use as low a heat as possible.

Seriously think about mixing things up with color and/ or highlighting! It's not necessarily a good thing to look just like you did five, ten, or twenty years ago. I look at my hair much like I do the walls of my house—a little primer, a little color, a little highlight, a little lowlight, and *voila*, perfect. (And if I grow tired of said perfect? Just prime back over and start again.)

Scan through hairstyle magazines or books; stop the woman who has a killer haircut and ask for the name of her stylist (get her name as well so you can reference the cut you'd like). Dare to assert your One Tough Mother personality and confidence with the follicles your momma gave you.

## Jewelry and Shoes

You know why I love these two items in particular? It rarely matters what weight I am for them to fit! And they can have me feeling sexy in a matter of seconds. There's probably a good chance your jewelry is piled up in a drawer somewhere or has been placed on a stuffed animal by a fashionista daughter. If so, gather up your stuff and take the time to create a place just for your necklaces, rings, bracelets, and watches. Don't make it harder than it is and don't feel like you have to go out and spend several hundred dollars on a jewelry armoire. (Then again, if you can . . . do!) Four years ago I purchased a couple of toile-covered jewelry drawers at Target and divided my earrings, rings, and bracelets into casual and dressy. I also lined a tie drawer with jewelry felt and made a place for some of my nicer pieces such as freshwater pearls. If you need to build up your jewelry inventory, look for major markdown sales at regional department stores and stop and shop at any Stein Mart with which you may be blessed to cross paths. (Don't even get me started on my Stein Mart testimony!) As with most things female, jewelry can be a fabulous outlet for individual creativity.

As for shoes . . . I grieve for the woman who has yet to discover their worth. Be it flip-flops, heels, or a retro pair of Vans as worn by the '82 surfer dude Jeff Spicoli (*Fast Times at Ridgemont High*), footwear is a never-ending source of sexy self-maintenance. Plus, you can go as cheap or as expensive as you want.

Now, for any moms reading this who find themselves with hard-to-fit feet, never fear, online resources can help: FootSmart.com offers choices in women's shoes from size 4.5 to 16. And one woman told me you just can't beat Payless Shoes for finding some of those hard-to-find widths and sizes. Another option is to visit a small, privately owned shoe store. These shopkeepers really want your business, and in most cases, they will do whatever they can do to get and keep that business! They will special order shoes for you—in the styles that you want. They may even be willing to contact other shoe stores to help you find what you are looking for if they aren't able to get it for you. You will also enjoy very personalized service in these types of stores that you won't find in the chain stores and discount stores—of course, you will pay for that service by paying a higher price for the shoes, unfortunately.

# Plastic Surgery

Once a year I get together with a group of raucous and deliciously real women. We pack a lot of conversations into a rather short period of time, and I don't believe there's much of anything that we haven't discussed, dissected, and deliberated about. They are a hoot, and all you need to know about them is summed up in the salutation I heard upon a late arrival two years ago. As they grabbed my luggage and hurried me into a kitchen teeming with food and other girls, Nancy looked at me and shouted, "Hey, Julie! Have you seen my new boobs? They're beautiful!"

Man, I like that. A woman unafraid to embrace her implants.

We can't have a talk about sexy without a little nip/tuck reality.

Let me throw out a disclaimer first: I'm not saying you have to have plastic surgery to be sexy. I'm not advocating blowing your chest up to double-F proportions. I'm not *underestimating* the power of exercise and diet (although I'm not the author to speak with authority on such matters either), and I'm not shallow.

I just got tired of my chest resting on my thighs.

And a friend or two of mine got tired of the freshly squeezed tube of toothpaste look of theirs.

A sixty-something One Tough Mother recently had her chin done.

And others have undergone a bit of liposuction reshaping.

It is what it is, girls, and it is nice to know there are options available when no amount of stomach crunches or wrinkle creams are going to do what you really want done. Be wise if you choose the surgical route (or noninvasive procedures such as chemical peels, dermabrasion, and thermage) and do your homework on the doctors you are considering. Take your time and consider the wise advice offered online by my plastic surgeon, Dr. Jean Loftus, at www.infoplasticsurgery.com.

Ask a friend: If a friend was satisfied with the care provided by a plastic surgeon, then chances are that you will be similarly pleased. Unfortunately, not everyone has a friend who has had plastic surgery.

Ask someone in the medical profession, such as your family doctor or a nurse: Keep in mind, however, that doctors and nurses may only be familiar with the physicians at their own hospitals, and they may refer to plastic surgeons based on personality or friendship rather than ability. They will also tend to refer to "hospital-based" plastic surgeons, who tend to perform mostly reconstructive surgery. Make sure your plastic surgeon spends most of his or her time performing cosmetic surgery—especially the one you seek.

Look for a Plastic Surgeon who is certified by the American Board of Plastic Surgery. Be aware of made-up boards that sound official and issue official-appearing certificates. These boards may sound impressive, but according to Joyce D. Nash, author of *What Your Doctor Can't Tell You About Cosmetic Surgery*, "Certification of competency from such organizations is probably meaningless." Be certain to ask from which board certification was received. If your plastic surgeon is not certified by the American Board of Plastic Surgery, be suspicious.

You may look in your telephone directory for a plastic surgeon, but beware: Know that in most metropolitan telephone directories, only about two thirds of the physicians listed under "Plastic and Reconstructive Surgeons" are plastic surgeons who are certified by the American Board of Plastic Surgery (ABPS). Some physicians listed in the plastic surgery section have absolutely no formal training in cosmetic plastic surgery.

Telephone directories in most states do not require physicians to state from which board they received certification. Therefore, physicians may advertise under "Plastic and Reconstructive Surgeons" and state they are board certified, but not be certified by the American Board of Plastic Surgery.

Look for a Plastic Surgeon who is a member of the American Society of Plastic Surgeons (ASPS). The ASPS only inducts plastic surgeons who are certified by the American Board of Plastic Surgery. To obtain the names of these plastic surgeons in your area, call the ASPS at 847-228-9900 or visit their web site at http://www.plasticsurgery.org.

Finding a qualified plastic surgeon may seem like a daunting task. It can be. Understand that unqualified physicians make great efforts to create the impression that they are plastic surgeons. Be aware that the term "board certified" is meaningless, unless it is associated with the name of the board from which certification was received. Know that, in many states, it is legal for unqualified physicians to perform plastic surgery procedures in which they have not been trained. Realize that you may unknowingly see an unqualified physician, but think he is a qualified plastic surgeon. If you understand these issues, then you are well ahead of the general public. To begin your search, call a reputable plastic surgery organization, such as the American Society of Plastic Surgeons (847-228-9900), ask for the names of plastic surgeons in your area, and carefully evaluate your plastic surgeon during the consultation.[2]

## Shapewear and Sexy Underwear

Okay, for those of us who have run out of plastic surgery funds or simply choose not to go under the knife, there is still hope. Never underestimate the power of the undergarment! Trust me, there is something for nearly everyone when it comes to hoisting, harnessing, and holding in parts that otherwise run amuck. Spanx by Sara Blakeley has your back—and front, and sides, and thighs, and arms—and is the closest thing to one-stop shapewear shopping you'll ever find (sizes S through XL). Click over to www.spanx.com and check out hosiery, tights, body shapers, bras, slimming intimates, and even T-shirts and maternity wear. You can also find Spanx in higher-end department stores everywhere. For those with a fuller figure, Just My Size is an online source for brand-name intimates and bras (up to size 58J!) plus full-figure fashions and more in sizes X to 6X, 14W to 40W! Find plus-size clothing in average, petite, and tall lengths at www.jms.com.

As for underwear, girls, it's time to throw out those nursing bras we discussed earlier as well as time to introduce something other than the sturdy cotton-panel panty to the intimates drawer in your bedroom.

Think red (or pink, or lime, or black—anything but cotton white)!

Think silky!

Think sexy!

Think matching bra and panties!

Oh, my. I hadn't owned such a thing for over fifteen years. My laundry basket was filled with Hanes for Her cotton numbers. Granted, I'd had the sexy bra thing going since 1992 (the year I had my breast reduction and entered the land of the perky and free), but matching panties had eluded me (and my husband) for years. I didn't see the light until speaking at a women's conference in fall 2003. I was interviewing another author who wrote of "the power of the red panty." I listened to her challenge six thousand women to pick up a pair (no matter the size), wear them under their everyday clothes, and just see if they didn't feel and act more sexy—better yet, she said, wear a matching set of red panties and bra and just see what happens.

Always one to take a challenge, I did just that. And boy-how-dee did the Get Sexy Back factor crank up a notch or two. (I was tempted to put a pair on my feet and wear another as a hat!) There's no definitive scientific research to prove what happens, but I guarantee you this: if you'll take the time to pick out a silky set that makes you feel feminine, something good is going to happen to you.

So there you have it, girls. No matter your height, weight, shoe size, body type, or skin color, you can be One Tough *and* Sexy Mother! Give yourself permission to spend a little more time, a little more money, and a lot more guilt-free thinking and action when it comes to doing what you need to stay that way.

# Notes

### Chapter 3: Sit Down and Shut Up

1. http://abcnews.go.com/GMA/AmericanFamily/story?id=2770170 &page=1>, January 2007.
2. Dr. James MacDonald, *Family Revival: God's Wisdom at My House*, audio CD.
3. Jennifer Rosenberg, "King Edward the VIII Abdicated for Love," About .com, http://history1900s.about.com/od/1930s/a/kingedward_3.htm.

### Chapter 6: Non, Nyet, Nada, Nein, Nulle

1. Jim Ellis, "Girl Kicked Off Plane After Tantrum," Breitbart.com, January 23, 2007, http://www.breitbart.com/news/2007/01/23/D8MR41C02.html.
2. Ibid.
3. William Sears, M.D., "18 Ways to Say 'No' Positively," AskDrSears.com, 2006, http://www.askdrsears.com/html/6/T061100.asp.
4. Bobbe Branch, "How to Say an Honest 'No,'" NW Parenting Consultants, http://www.geocities.com/nwparentingconsultants/HonestNO.html.
5. Betsy Hart, *It Takes a Parent* (New York: G. P. Putnam's Sons, 2005), 136.
6. Ibid., 123.
7 . Ibid., 131.

### Chapter 8: Truly, Madly, Deeply

1. "Storm Proof Your Marriage," www.walkintheword.com/WeeklyWalk_ View.aspx?weeklywalk=3/, January, 2007.

## Chapter 10: Just Say It

1. Susan Alexander Yates, "Praying for Your Kids: 5 Easy Ways to Get Started," *Today's Christian Woman* 24, no. 3 (May/June 2002), 18. Available online at http://www.christianitytoday.com/tcw/2002/003/12.18.html.
2. "Prayers for Children," AllAboutPrayer.org, http://www.allaboutprayer .org/prayers-for-children-faq.htm.

## Chapter 11: My Kingdom for a Slingshot

1. Beth Moore, *Praying God's Word* (Nashville: Broadman & Holman, 2000), 3.
2. Terri Mauro, "Beware of Lindane," About.com, http://specialchildren .about.com/od/medicalissues/a/lindane.htm.
3. Amy Fackler, M.A., "Lindane for Lice," WebMD.com, December 28, 2004, http://children.webmd.com/Lindane-for-lice.
4. Used with permission. Lindsey O'Connor, "Fear Factor," *MOMSense* mini 2005.

## Chapter 12: You're Only a Failure If You Quit, Like, Forever

1. Jane Johnson Struck, "Carla's Quest," *Today's Christian Parenting*, Spring 2005, accessed online at http://www.christianitytoday.com/cpt/2005/001/16.34 .html, July 2006.

## Appendix: Maintaining and Accessorizing "The Package"

1. "Antibiotic Acne Treatment," Acne Talks, http://www.acnetalks.com/ pimple/Acne-Treatment/Methods/Antibiotic-Acne-Treatment.htm.
2. Used with permission. Dr. Jean M. Loftus, "Finding a Plastic Surgeon," InfoPlasticSurgery.com, http://www.infoplasticsurgery.com/findsurgeon .html.

# Acknowledgments

There are two "best parts" to any book-writing experience (in my humble opinion). The first being able to say "I wrote a book." Wrote, as in past tense—done, finished, kaput, el finished. See, I'm a speaker who writes. I'm energized, and my creativity is sparked by relational and conversational interactions with live audiences and one-on-one moments of connection with individuals. I find the actual, solitary discipline of writing to be a most difficult and lonely process, and it hasn't been unusual for friends and family members to observe me staring blankly at a glaring monitor screen while drooling and mumbling incoherently about "stupid transitional phrases" for months on end.

As such, it's always nice to get to this the second part: being able to record for posterity's sake a mighty THANK YOU shout-out to those who put up with my (admittedly) incessant mumbling and writing angst. As well as kudos to all who helped make this, my seventh book in seven years, not only a publishing possibility but a really great book in the process.

*Rick, Kristen, Ricky Neal, and Patrick.* Without you, I'd be a writer without stories and a wife and mom tossed about without the four anchors that keep her tethered to grace, love, real life, and what is truly—in the light of eternity—important.

*Beth Lagerborg and Elisa Morgan (MOPS International)*. From a businesslike getting-to-know-you meeting in 2001 to cackling laughter, late-night room service calls, and joining forces to create a raucously real book real moms will love and appreciate—whew, it's been an amazing few years. Thank you for believing and hearing the message of *One Tough Mother* and allowing me the privilege of working alongside an organization that loves to equip moms to reach their incredible mothering potential.

*Esther Fedorkevich*. For fourteen months I waited for a literary agent. But not just any agent—I waited (and prayed for) a savvy, well-connected, manager/agent who saw the Big Picture when it came to what I would be doing as a writer, speaker, entertainer, and (please, oh, please!) radio host. And I wanted said agent to be a woman. You have not because you ask not, right? Well, I asked, and God graced me with this dynamo who more than met my requirements.

Going before this author is a bevy of editorial, marketing, and PR staff at Revell: *Jennifer Leep, Acquisitions Editor; Kristin Kornoelje, Assistant Managing Editor; Cheryl Van Andel, Senior Art Director; Twila Bennett, Senior Marketing Director; Suzie Cross, Assistant Marketing Manager; Deonne Beron, Publicity Manager; Brooke Nolen, Senior Publicist; and Claudia Marsh, Broadcast and Online Publicist*.

If my transitional phrases make sense . . . all the thanks go to Jennifer and Kristin.

If the cover grabs your eye . . . all the thanks go to Cheryl.

If you see or hear about me and *One Tough Mother* in magazines, radio broadcasts, publishing papers, or if you catch me and my book online via advertisements and interviews . . . all the thanks go to Twila, Suzie, Deonne, Brooke, and Claudia.

And should you meet me and realize I actually look like the title cover shot . . . well, all the thanks and praise goes to the fabulous Vicki Taufer, owner and photographer extraordinaire of V Gallery in Morton, IL (www.vgallery.net). I requested the "long and lean" photo lens—she did the best she could.

**Julie Barnhill** is a popular speaker and the bestselling author of *She's Gonna Blow! Real Help for Moms Dealing with Anger*, as well as several other popular books that tap into the "everyday themes of everyday people." She has appeared on *Oprah*, NBC's *The Other Half*, CNN, and other national and regional programs. She lives in Prairie City, Illinois, with her family.

If you're interested in Julie as a keynote speaker for your next event, you can email her office online at: julie@ juliebarnhill.

# The MOPS Story

You take care of your children, mom. Who takes care of you? MOPS International (Mothers of Preschoolers) encourages, equips, and develops mothers of preschoolers to be the best moms they can be.

MOPS is dedicated to the message that "mothering matters" and understands that moms of young children need encouragement during these critical and formative years. Chartered MOPS groups meet in approximately in 4,000 churches and Christian ministries throughout the United States and 24 other countries. Each MOPS group helps mothers find friendship and acceptance, provides opportunities for women to develop and practice leadership skills in a group, and promotes spiritual growth. MOPS groups are chartered ministries of local churches and meet at a variety of times and locations: daytime, evenings, and on weekends; in churches, homes, and workplaces.

The MOPPETS program offers a loving, learning experience for children while their moms attend MOPS. Other quality MOPS resources include MOMSense magazine, MOPS books available at the www.MOPShop.org, web site forums, and events.

With 14.3 million mothers of preschoolers in the United States alone, many moms can't attend a MOPS group. However, these moms still need the mothering support that MOPS International can offer! For a small registration fee, any mother of a preschooler can join the MOPS International Membership and receive MOMSense magazine (6 times a year), a weekly MOM-E-Mail of encouragement, and other valuable benefits.

Get Connected!
www.MOPS.org